The Great Commission for Today

David M. Howard

InterVarsity Press
Downers Grove
Illinois 60515

other books by David M. Howard

Words of Fire, Rivers of Tears
By the Power of the Holy Spirit
How Come, God?
Student Power in World Evangelism
The Costly Harvest

InterVarsity Press is the book publishing division of Inter-Varsity Christian Fellowship, a student movement active on campus at hundreds of universities, colleges and schools of nursing. For information about local and regional activities, write IVCF, 233 Langdon St., Madison, WI 53703.

ISBN 0-87784-646-4
Library of Congress Catalog Card Number: 76-12302

Printed in the United States of America

CHRISTIAN HERITAGE COLLEGE
BY HIM ALL THINGS CONSIST
SAN DIEGO, CALIFORNIA 1970
CHRISTIAN
HERITAGE
COLLEGE
LIBRARY

To my brother Phil who from
early childhood
has been a friend and
an example
in pointing me to God

acknowledgments

I am indebted to President Vernon Grounds and Professor Ralph Covell of the Conservative Baptist Theological Seminary in Denver, Colorado, for the invitation in 1975 to deliver the David Kraft Memorial Lectureship in Missions. The friendship and warm response of students and faculty at the Seminary encouraged me to expand these lectures into book form.

Kay Barton, my assistant in Inter-Varsity Christian Fellowship, was responsible for typing the manuscript, checking all Scripture quotations, and helping in the editing. Her efficient work has made my job immeasurably more enjoyable.

The enthusiastic response of students throughout the United States and Canada to a biblical approach to missions has honed my thinking and encouraged me further to search the Word of God in order to understand what our Lord wishes to tell us today about our responsibility to the world.

Contents

Foreword

As I have traveled to remote corners of the world, I have been overwhelmed again and again by the needs of most of mankind. Material needs beyond description. Spiritual needs beyond measure. Literally billions of people are hungry—hungry for physical bread and hungry for spiritual bread, the eternal Bread of Life.

I have also been impressed with the opportunities that await the church, opportunities to proclaim the gospel of our Lord and to have that gospel heard and received. In evangelistic meetings in many countries I have seen men and women of diverse cultures respond with faith to the message of salvation and hope found only in Christ Jesus.

Yet the need for capable and committed Christian workers is greater than ever before. From every nation and culture, the church needs men and women of faith who have a solid understanding of Scripture, who are sensitive to the differences between societies and who can communicate the gospel fully and clearly.

Dave Howard is one of the few people in the church today who can write knowledgeably from several perspectives. He has served as a missionary and sees the task from the viewpoint of the field worker. He has been deeply involved with students, motivating them to become active witnesses of their faith, and he knows the questions that young people have about the relevance of evangelism. He is also a mission administrator, concerned with the needs of organizations and with relationships to churches and constituents.

This book speaks to each of these groups.

In clear, simple language he shows the scriptural foundation of the Great Commission and brings together the "whole counsel" of Scripture on this vital teaching. This proclamation is not a single act, Dave points out. It must be coupled with service: "Our understanding of the gospel is deficient unless we see it as ministering to all of creation. Preaching must be accompanied by practical application of the gospel in daily life."

In our day when so much of the church seems to lack the energy and vision for evangelism and when so many do not really believe in the lostness of mankind apart from Christ, Dave Howard shows us the many facets of the Great Commission and how essential a part of church life it must be.

Michael Green, describing the motivation of the early Christians, wrote, "They had an unquenchable conviction that Jesus was the key to life and death, happiness and purpose, and they simply could not keep quiet about him. The Spirit of Jesus drove them into mission."

It is my prayer that this same Spirit of Jesus will use this book to drive more Christians into that same mission: sharing the good news of Jesus Christ with a world that does not yet know him.

W. Stanley Mooneyham
President
World Vision International

preface

During the late 1960s and early 1970s students throughout North America were reacting negatively to the idea of "missions," especially when defined as overseas efforts. This was all part of the atmosphere of the times. There were strong reactions in the student world against many things: government, families, "the establishment," the church and society in general. The idea of "missions" thus came in for its share of criticism.

Some of this reaction was legitimate and healthy. It forced the church to evaluate anew its responsibilities to the world and sharpen its understanding of its mission. On the other hand, some of it was based on misunderstanding or ignorance of what the Word of God says. But as I travel throughout North America now, I find that honest Christian students invariably respond in a positive way when they understand what God says to us about the mission of the church in the world today. Obedience to the Word of God becomes the issue rather than a reaction to a false image or preconceived notion about "foreign missions" or "missionaries." And when obedience is the issue, the response is positive among those who genuinely wish to follow Jesus Christ. I am encouraged with the number of students today who want to do just that.

The Great Commission passages of the New Testament may well be among the most familiar yet least understood parts of the Bible. It is easy to quote a familiar verse such as Mark 16:15 ("Go into all the world and preach the gospel to the whole creation") without realizing its tremendous scope and far-reaching implications. This book is an attempt to show that the Great Commission is part of the warp and woof of the gospel and that it has deep significance for discipleship. Without it the gospel is incomplete.

This study of the Great Commission as given in each of the four Gospels and Acts will focus on two aspects of the Commission. First, I will note the chronological sequence of the various times Jesus Christ gave the Commission. A close study reveals that he gave the Great Commission not just once but actually three times or possibly more. There is some very significant truth to be noted in the various ways Christ presented this great command.

Second, I will look at the context, that is, how the Commission is given in each book and relates to the message of that book. Each of the Gospel writers had a specific picture of Jesus Christ. Matthew shows him as the King, Mark as the Servant of the Lord, Luke as the Son of Man and John as the Son of God. There is a definite connection between how Jesus is presented by the writer and how Christ gave the Commission in that book.

This is not a book primarily for scholars. Rather it is written for Christians who honestly want to seek God's will for their lives and understand the implications of discipleship. Detailed and critical studies of the texts can be found elsewhere. It is hoped that this treatment of the Scriptures will help students and others to see more clearly the meaning of the Great Commission for today.

— *David M. Howard*

1

And they rose that same hour and returned to Jerusalem; and they found the eleven gathered together and those who were with them, who said, "The Lord has risen indeed, and has appeared to Simon!" Then they told what had happened on the road, and how he was known to them in the breaking of the bread.

As they were saying this, Jesus himself stood among them. But they were startled and frightened, and supposed that they saw a spirit. And he said to them, "Why are you troubled, and why do questionings rise in your hearts? See my hands and my feet, that it is I myself; handle me, and see; for a spirit has not flesh and bones as you see that I have." And while they still disbelieved for joy, and wondered, he said to them, "Have you anything here to eat?" They gave him a piece of broiled fish, and he took it and ate before them.

Then he said to them, "These are my words which I spoke to you, while I was still with you, that everything written about me in the law of Moses and the prophets and the psalms must be fulfilled." Then he opened their minds to understand the Scriptures, and said to them, "Thus it is written, that the Christ should suffer and on the third day rise from the dead, and that repentance and forgiveness of sins should be preached in his name to all nations, beginning from Jerusalem. You are witnesses of these things. And behold, I send the promise of my Father upon you; but stay in the city, until you are clothed with power from on high."

Luke 24:33-49

The Son of Man Brings the Commission into Focus

We walk with two men down the road to Emmaus. The discussion centers around the recent execution of a certain Jesus of Nazareth in Jerusalem and the startling reports that he has been seen alive. Jesus (who seems to be a stranger) meets them on the afternoon of the resurrection day and asks them what they are talking about. Is it possible that there is someone who still doesn't know about all these things? After listening to their account, Jesus opens the Scriptures to them and explains the meanings of the prophecies concerning himself. After going home with them, he reveals himself to them and then disappears. They return to the city of Jerusalem and tell the other disciples who were gathered together that evening that they have seen the Lord.

While they meet together Jesus himself suddenly stands in their midst. The disciples are understandably terrified. They think it is a spirit. They can't grasp the fact that he is alive in bodily form. So he proves to them that he is. "Don't you see my hands and my feet? Don't you see that this is really me? Touch me if you want to. That will show you I am real. Ghosts don't have flesh and bones." But the disciples still wondered if they weren't seeing things, disbelieving for joy. So he asks them for something to eat. They offer a piece of fish and he eats it! Ghosts don't eat food. This must be their Master!

Having convinced them that he is alive, Jesus begins to explain the meaning of the things that have taken place. "What I am going to tell you now is actually the same thing I've told you during the last three years. Everything that is prophecied about me in the books of Moses, the prophets and the psalms must come to pass." So he helps them understand what the Scriptures were really saying about him. "It says in the Scriptures that the Messiah has to suffer. But he will rise to life after being dead for three days. Because of this, the word should be proclaimed in his name to every nation on earth that if people will turn to God from their old sinful ways, he will forgive them. And Jerusalem is the place to begin. You have all seen these very things happen. But look, I'll pass on my Father's promise to help you. Stay in the city until you receive power from heaven."

This is a tense moment. It is the first time that Jesus Christ has met with his disciples as a group since before the crucifixion. The last time he was with them was in the Garden of Gethsemane. At that time "they all forsook him, and fled" (Mk. 14:50). Although he has seen a few individuals during the course of the day, what do you suppose he is going to say to them now as a group? We might assume that Jesus would reprimand them. He might well look back to their cowardice in the Garden of Gethsemane, asking why they left him at the moment of his great crisis. Instead, he links together what he has done up to this point with what their responsibility will be from now on.

Beginning with Moses

Jesus does not open his discourse with the Great Commission

itself. Rather, he starts with Moses, the prophets and the psalms. He goes back and explains all that has happened as part of the whole history of God's redemptive plan. This is similar to what he had done that afternoon on the way to Emmaus. Now that evening as he meets with the group of eleven disciples he again begins with Moses. He continues right through the prophets and the psalms explaining the significance of the things that have happened. He was preparing to give them their responsibility through the Commission.

Where do you suppose he went in the books of Moses and the psalms and the prophets? It would be fascinating had the Holy Spirit led Luke to give us a fuller record of what Jesus said. We can only let our imagination run a bit. But I don't feel it would be running too far to pick out a few of the elements in the Old Testament that Jesus quite possibly emphasized.

Since he began with the books of Moses, he almost certainly started in Genesis. In fact, I would dare to guess that he started in Genesis 1. J. H. Bavinck, a great Dutch missionary-theologian, makes a thought-provoking statement when he points out that Genesis 1:1 is obviously the necessary basis of the Great Commission as given in the Gospels.[1] What is the connection between Genesis 1:1 and the Great Commission? The more I thought about what Bavinck pointed out, the more I saw the great truth there.

This verse is so well known that sometimes we miss its significance. "In the beginning God created the heavens and the earth." That means that everything God created is within his sphere of interest. God did not create anything in which he is not interested. God created the heavens and the earth. Therefore, *all* the heavens and the earth and everything in the heavens and earth—including every man and woman that he ever created—concern him.

Therefore, when Jesus Christ told his disciples to go to all nations, to every creation, to all parts of the world, he rests on the fact that all parts of the world are part of God's creation. What God has made is good and God is interested in it. As the Creator he owns what he has made. Therefore, he has a right and a reason to be involved. He desires all of his possessions to be within his sphere of activity.

Jesus might have continued in that chapter. He might have pointed out the first command ever given to mankind, found immediately after the story of the creation: "And God blessed them, and God said to them, 'Be fruitful and multiply, and fill the earth and subdue it; and have dominion over the fish of the sea and over the birds of the air and over every living thing that moves upon the earth' " (Gen. 1:28). Why fill the earth? Because all the earth is part of God's realm.

If everything that God made is good, then no part of the creation is to be neglected. Since man is made in the image of God and is given dominion over all the earth, the sphere of man's activity is to be the entire world. This is true of the physical world of nature. It is also true of the political and geographical realms of the world, which will be discussed later. So Bavinck's linking of Genesis 1:1 with the Commission is a correct understanding of the implications of the doctrine of creation.

As the story proceeds we read of rebellion and of the Fall. Things move from bad to worse. Finally God says, "I've had enough! I will wipe out the human race and start over again with one family." And so we have the story of the flood. The human race is destroyed with the exception of Noah's family. What was the first thing God said to Noah when he came out of the ark? The flood is over. The waters have abated. The ark has settled down. Noah comes out and God speaks to him. "And God blessed Noah and his sons, and said to them, 'Be fruitful and multiply, and fill the earth' " (Gen. 9:1). What is he saying? "My plans haven't changed. What I said to Adam I am saying to you. Start over now. I want the whole earth to be filled. Noah, you do what I told Adam to do." The command has not changed.

But history moves on. Again we read of man's rebellion. Once again things go from bad to worse. By the time we get into chapters ten and eleven of Genesis, man's rebellion against God has again become critical. In chapter eleven we find that fascinating story of the Tower of Babel:

> Now the whole earth had one language and few words. And as men migrated from the east, they found a plain in the land of Shinar and settled there. And they said to one another, "Come, let us make bricks, and burn them thoroughly."
>
> And they had brick for stone, and bitumen for mortar. Then they said, "Come, let us build ourselves a city, and a tower with its top in the heavens, and let us make a name for ourselves, lest we be scattered abroad upon the face of the whole earth." (Gen. 11:1-4)

If you ask why the Tower of Babel was built, nine times out of ten the average person will say, "To reach up into heaven." This is no doubt based on the statement, "let us build . . . a tower with its top in the heavens." But the real reason is stated very clearly. "Let us make a name for ourselves, lest we be scattered abroad upon the face of the whole earth." They built the Tower of Babel as a place of unity, a rallying point where they could come together. There was security in unity in the face of the unknown dangers of the unpopulated earth. In a sense they said, "We do *not* want to be scattered abroad upon the face of the whole earth. We will *not* obey the first command of God."

God says, "Yes you will." And God has a very effective way of producing this. There are many ways he could have chosen to scatter mankind. I can't think of a more effective way than the one he chose. He simply confused their language.

Have you ever tried to get along for any length of time in

another land or culture whose language you did not know? I have done this on more than one occasion. In high school and college I studied five years of French and ended up going to Latin America. I do not recommend that as the best preparation! I did not know one word of Spanish. On the plane en route to Costa Rica I learned two words—*No comprendo* meaning "I do not understand." I remembered those two words and used them frequently during my first months in Costa Rica.

Many years later I went to Europe for the first time. Now the tables were turned when I traveled in France and other French-speaking areas. My high school and college French had long since been crowded back into the dim recesses of my mind, and I was unable to reconstruct it adequately. When I tried to speak a phrase in French, Spanish seemed to come out automatically. This didn't make for the best communication. While it is enjoyable to travel for a while in an area where we do not know the language, the novelty soon wears off. Either we learn to communicate or we go elsewhere.

God did a very effective thing by confusing the language. Sooner or later they simply had to split up. The first outward movements of the human race in fulfillment of God's command came at God's initiative. God forced the issue when mankind was refusing to obey.

To the End of the Earth

We find an interesting parallel in the New Testament. Jesus Christ, in the first chapter of Acts, gave the plan of how the gospel was to be spread. He said, "But you shall receive power when the Holy Spirit has come upon you; and you shall be my witnesses in Jerusalem and in all Judea and Samaria and to the end of the earth" (Acts 1:8). The first seven chapters of Acts indicate that the apostles did a good job of obeying the first part of that Commission. They did witness faithfully in Jerusalem. They stood up and boldly gave the Word. They were thrown in prison because of it. But we read nothing about Judea and Samaria. What was happening? They hadn't really caught on yet. They were not fully obeying that Commission.

So once again the issue was forced. God permitted a persecution to come after the stoning of Stephen. "They were all scattered throughout the region of Judea and Samaria. . . . Those who were scattered went about preaching the word" (Acts 8:1, 4). They were scattered to the very places Jesus had told them to go and to which they hadn't gone! This still happens today from time to time. God permits persecution or perhaps some kind of tragedy to force the issue.

Some years ago I came in contact with an Indian from the jungles of Colombia whose name was Isaiah (not his original name, but one he chose from the Bible when he became a Christian). I asked him how he came to Christ. He said, "Don David, do you know Don Ricardo Velez?"

I said, "Yes, I know Don Ricardo Velez."

He said, "Well, he led me to Christ."

My mind flashed back. Ricardo Velez had been a pastor in southern Colombia during the years of violent persecution through which the church had passed in the 1950s and the early part of the 1960s. He had suffered physically. When I knew Don Ricardo, he was a middle-aged man with a bald head. He had a scar that ran from the middle of his forehead down to the back of his skull. His whole head had been laid open with a machete blow in one attack. Another time he was badly chopped up with a machete and left for dead. Twice more he was beaten up. Finally he decided that perhaps it was wiser to get out of that area and he did.

He and a group of believers found their way through the mountains and jungles up into northern Colombia. They settled down, purchased small plots of ground and began to farm and to witness. They built a little chapel. As people came in from the surrounding area, they witnessed to them about Jesus Christ.

One day Isaiah came down from a totally unevangelized area up the San Jorge River. He came into that little chapel and Ricardo Velez led him to Christ. When I first met Isaiah, he was already evangelizing his own tribe where no missionary or pastor had ever gone. Ricardo Velez and his friends had been scattered by persecution from southern Colombia up to northern Colombia. The result was that the gospel was now reaching to areas where it had never gone before. God will sometimes permit Christians to be persecuted for his own purposes. The first outward movements of the human race and even of the Christian church came at the initiative of God himself.

Perhaps Christ went on and took them to Genesis 12. He may have showed them the call of Abraham, pointing out how God focused on one man through whom he was going to build a family, then a nation. God's purpose was not solely for that one man, not solely for that family, not solely for that nation, but that "by you *all the families of the earth* shall bless themselves" (Gen. 12:3 my emphasis). From the very beginning of Israel's call as a nation, it was for the sake of all families of the earth. The worldwide emphasis was clear.

Jesus Christ may then have gone into the historical books and showed them how God frequently did something for Israel but with a broader purpose. For instance, after the crossing of the Red Sea and the crossing of the Jordan River, Joshua said, "For the Lord your God dried up the waters of the Jordan for you until you passed over, as the Lord your God did to the Red Sea, which he dried up for us until we passed over, so *that all the peoples of the earth may know that the hand of the LORD is mighty;* that you may fear the LORD your God for ever" (Josh. 4:23-24, my emphasis).

When David had his confrontation with Goliath he grasped

the larger significance of what God wanted to do. He said,

> You come to me with a sword and with a spear and with a javelin; but I come to you in the name of the Lord of hosts, the God of the armies of Israel, whom you have defied. This day the Lord will deliver you into my hand, and I will strike you down, and cut off your head; and I will give the dead bodies of the host of the Philistines this day to the birds of the air and to the wild beasts of the earth; *that all the earth may know that there is a God in Israel*. (1 Sam. 17:45-46, my emphasis)

Jesus took them into the psalms and into the prophets. While the prophets spoke specifically to Israel, the worldwide emphasis was never absent. Go through the prophets and you will find repeatedly that God's interest is that all mankind might come to himself.

In the psalms he might have showed them Psalm 96. In picking a theme for Urbana 76, Inter-Varsity Christian Fellowship's Student Missionary Convention, a phrase directly out of Psalm 96 was chosen: "Declare his glory among the nations." The glory of God is a central thrust of all missionary effort. "Among the nations" emphasizes the worldwide outreach that is involved in this effort. "Declare" speaks of personal responsibility.

As he went through the Old Testament he was saying, "Now look, beginning in the law of Moses and all through the books of history and the psalms and the prophets, this is what God has been preparing. What I have been doing is part of the whole history of redemption." The Great Commission is not an isolated text picked out to be set apart and used at missionary conferences. The Great Commission is warp and woof of the redemptive history of God from the beginning to the end. Jesus Christ wanted his disciples to see that truth. Only after doing this was he prepared to commission his disciples with their responsibility.

Jesus . . . Son of Adam

Before moving on, let's consider how Luke 24 fits in with the rest of the book. Luke presents Jesus Christ as the Son of Man. There are a number of characteristics which make this clear.

For example, take the genealogies. There are only two genealogies of Christ given in the New Testament—one in Matthew and one in Luke. The one in Matthew starts with Abraham because Matthew depicts Jesus as the King of the Jews. But the genealogy in Luke starts with Adam because Luke presents Jesus as the Son of Man.

Only these two of the four Gospel writers take time to describe the birth of Jesus Christ. When John presents him as the Son of God, the story of his physical birth is not necessary to develop the main theme. Mark, whose Gospel is filled with action, likewise bypasses the nativity as not essential to his purposes.

But Luke tells the story of the birth in far greater detail than even Matthew. In fact, he spends three long chapters on the birth and its surrounding significance, Jesus' early childhood and the beginning of his ministry. He does this because he is talking about the Son of Man. It is essential to give his background to understand his human origins.

Luke also describes what Jesus did at the beginning of his ministry. In Luke 4 Jesus went into Nazareth where he had grown up. He entered the synagogue on the Sabbath where they gave him the scroll to read. He stood up, turned to the book of Isaiah and read a great prophecy about himself. Why did he pick this prophecy? Because it shows the ministry that he is going to have as a man—man to man. The prophecy says, "The Spirit of the Lord is upon me, because he has anointed me to preach good news to the poor. He has sent me to proclaim release to the captives and recovering of sight to the blind, to set at liberty those who are oppressed, to proclaim the acceptable year of the Lord" (Lk. 4:18-19). That is his ministry according to Luke: to minister to those in need—the blind that they might have sight, the captives that they might be set free, the oppressed that they might be liberated from their oppression—to minister to the human needs of mankind. So the Son of Man said, "I have come as a man to meet the needs of my fellow man. I am going to proclaim the acceptable year of the Lord."

Luke also has a great emphasis on prayer. We observe more about the prayer life of Jesus Christ in Luke than in any other Gospel. (Lk. 3:21—praying at time of baptism; 5:16—the withdrawing into the wilderness to pray; 6:12—praying all night just before choosing the disciples; 9:18—praying alone just before Peter's great confession; 9:28—praying at the time of the Transfiguration; 11:1—praying just before he taught the disciples the Lord's prayer; 22:41—praying in Gethsemane.) Repeatedly in Luke we see Jesus withdrawing to spend a night in prayer or going out in the wilderness to pray. Why? Because as a man he saw his need of God. And as the Son of Man, he was conscious of his dependence on God, his Father.

To Other Cities Also

Luke also shows Jesus emphasizing the universality of reaching out to mankind. This is seen geographically as well as socially and culturally. Let's look first at geography.

In Luke 4, Jesus has gone to Capernaum where the early part of his ministry seemed to be centered. There he began to preach with authority, to teach and to heal. They brought him the sick and he healed them. He went into the house of Simon and healed his mother-in-law. In the evening they brought him those with various diseases, and he healed them all. Then we read, "And when it was day he departed and went into a lonely place. And the people sought him and came to him, and would have kept him from leaving them" (Lk. 4:42).

Apparently they got the impression that he was about to

leave them. He had just barely begun his ministry. We don't know how long he had been there, but it was probably not very long. Some disciples had come to him; some were believing in him. He had healed some people, but there was a lot more to be done. You can imagine what the people might have said when they saw that he was about to go. "Now wait a minute. You don't mean to say that you are going to leave Capernaum! You have hardly started. This city is still full of all kinds of corruption. You can't leave here now. Just look at all the corruption there is in government! Look at all the poverty, all the oppression, all the sinfulness, all the disease. You haven't cleaned it all up. Don't leave."

How did Jesus reply? At the outset of his ministry to show what his purposes were, he said to them, "I must preach the good news of the kingdom of God *to the other cities also*; for I was sent for this purpose" (Lk. 4:43, my emphasis). He was saying, "I cannot stay in one place. My ministry is to all mankind. I must go to the other cities also. I was sent for this purpose." But don't think that didn't rend his heart.

I have had the privilege on just a few occasions to be the first missionary ever to go to certain little villages in Colombia. I have watched with joy as new believers began to get into the Scriptures. It was thrilling to sit down with them and try to teach them for the first time in their lives what Christianity is all about. These were areas where no missionary or pastor lived. I lived in the city and traveled out to these areas spending a week or two at a time teaching. Eventually I would have to leave and return to my family and the other responsibilities that God had given me.

I can remember getting ready to leave some remote village in the jungles and having these people come to me and say, "You mean you are leaving now? How can you leave? There is no one else here that knows the Scriptures. Most of us don't even know how to read. How can you possibly leave us? There is no pastor, no missionary." Don't think that doesn't tear the heart out of a person. If that tore my heart, how much more must the heart of Jesus Christ been torn when they said to him in Capernaum, "You mean you are leaving now? How can you leave?" Jesus Christ had to say to them, "I have other sheep, that are not of this fold; I must bring them also" (Jn. 10:16). The gospel must keep spreading. We cannot stop in any one spot.

Across Society's Boundaries

Jesus moved out to all elements of society. He did not spend all his time with the sick and poor. Look through Luke and see the people to whom he ministered.

Three times in Luke he went into the home of a Pharisee to dine (Lk. 7:36; 11:37; 14:1). One time a sinful woman came and broke an alabaster flask and anointed his feet (Lk. 7:36-50). They said, "If he only knew what kind of a woman that was, he would never let her touch him." He ministered to the outcast, the stricken and the sinful as well as to the high class religious leaders.

Then he went into the home of the Publicans—the hated people. He was invited for dinner to the home of Levi, a tax collector (Lk. 5:27-32). He invited himself into the home of Zacchaeus, another hated tax collector (Lk. 19:1-10). These men had sold their souls to Rome and were despised by their fellow countrymen. Yet Jesus went and ministered to them because he loved them.

As we have seen, he reached out to the poor and the oppressed. All through Luke there is that emphasis which Christ himself brought up at the beginning: "I have come to call the poor and set them at liberty."

Dr. M. C. Tenney points out that there are seven parables given exclusively in Luke which are concerned with the contrast of poverty and wealth or which stress economic need: the two debtors (7:41-43), the friend at midnight (11:5-8), the rich man and his barns (12:13-21), the lost coin (15:8-10), the clever steward (16:1-13), the unjust judge and the importunate widow (18:1-8).[2]

He reached out to the rich as well. Zacchaeus was probably a well-to-do man. Joseph of Arimathea must have been a man of some means. Somewhere Jesus ministered to him and had an influence on him.

There is also a great emphasis on women in the book of Luke, more than in any other Gospel. Women are mentioned forty-three times in Luke and only forty-nine times in Matthew and Mark put together.

Luke often mentions children too. There are several cases where Jesus specifically ministered to them. (Lk. 7:11-17—raising the son of the widow of Nain; 9:37-43—casting an unclean spirit out of a child; 9:46-48—using a child as an example of being greatest.)

Across Cultural and Religious Boundaries

Jesus also cut across cultures. He reached out to the Samaritans, those despised half-Jews with whom the Jews had no dealings. In fact, he even made them heroes at times. He once told a story in which he could have made anyone he wanted the hero. He told of the man on the road to Jericho beaten by thieves and left to die. A Jewish priest came by. That priest could have well been the hero, but he turned away. A Levite came by, and he could have been the hero. But he also passed by on the other side. Jesus makes another man the hero. He tells about the Samaritan who came along and bound up that man's wounds. Can't you imagine the Pharisees grinding their teeth? "Look, he made up that story. Why does he make a Samaritan the hero?" Simply because he wanted it very clear, "I love Samaritans as well as I love Jews" (Lk. 10:29-37).

Luke relates the story of ten lepers who were healed. Nine

of them went their way and only one came back to say thank you. Luke adds in parenthesis one little phrase that might seem totally irrelevant to the story. He says about this man, "He was a Samaritan" (Lk. 17:11-19).

The Jews, of course, thought the Gentiles were outside the sphere of God's love and activity. They had no relationship to Jehovah of Israel. But Jesus demonstrated his love for Gentiles. One day a centurion came to him. He was a leader of the Roman guard that kept Israel under control, the one who was in charge of maintaining law and order. He said to Jesus, "Will you come? My servant is ill. But you don't even have to come to my house. I am unworthy that you should come under my roof. Just say the word and he will be healed." Jesus turned to that Roman Gentile and said, "Not even in Israel have I found such faith" (Lk. 7:9).

As the Son of Man, Jesus demonstrates his love to all mankind. He cuts across geographic boundaries, not just remaining in Capernaum but moving out to other cities also. He shows his love to every element of society as well, be they religious leaders, hated outcasts, women, children, rich, poor, Pharisees, Publicans. And lastly, he moves across cultural and religious boundaries to reach out to the Samaritans and the Gentiles. Geography, society, culture or religion cannot limit his love.

You Are Witnesses of These Things

With that as a background for the book of Luke and having seen how Jesus traced the great redemptive history from the beginning, let's look at the Commission itself.

> Thus it is written, that the Christ should suffer and on the third day rise from the dead, and that repentance and forgiveness of sins should be preached in his name to all nations, beginning from Jerusalem. You are witnesses of these things. (Lk. 24: 46-48)

First, he summarizes the gospel as centering around his death and resurrection. Those are the basic facts. Then he summarizes what the response must be. There must be repentance from sin. On the basis of that repentance God responds with forgiveness. This is the heart of the gospel.

So repentance and forgiveness of sins must be preached. Where? Among all nations. The groundwork had been laid from the beginning of the book when he said, "I must go to those other cities also." Now when he says to his disciples, "You must go to all nations," they could get the point. He had been building this into them and giving them an example to follow throughout his own ministry.

Having told them where the gospel is to be proclaimed, he says, "You are witnesses of these things." That is, "You are the ones who are to do the job." Although this was given specifically to the eleven disciples, there can be no question that this applies to the whole church of Jesus Christ. The entire context of the New Testament is that this responsibility relates to every believer wherever or whoever he may be.

The history of missions and a study of the New Testament church show that whenever the gospel spreads rapidly, it is because every Christian has accepted his responsibility to be a witness. The old gap between clergy and laity is nowhere to be found in Scripture when it comes to witnessing. "You are witnesses of these things."

I was in a rural village in Colombia one time called Thyatira. (That was not the original name. When whole villages became Christian in a great people movement, sometimes they would change the name of their village to a biblical one.) There were about one hundred believers in Thyatira at a Bible conference.

One day in a Bible study I asked, "How many of you came to Christ through the ministry of a missionary or a pastor?"

Not one hand went up.

I said, "How many of you came to Christ because a neighbor or friend told you about Jesus Christ?"

One hundred hands went up! You see what was happening? The gospel was spreading because everyone had accepted this responsibility to be a witness. These people were not relying on a group of "clergy" to carry out the Great Commission. They knew it was the responsibility of every Christian, and they acted on it.

Jesus Christ says, "This is your responsibility. Now wait until you are clothed with power from on high." We will discuss later the promise of the coming of the Holy Spirit. But it is significant to note that he gave that promise the first time he gave the Commission.

What does this teaching in Luke have to do with us? Simply this. First, as we look at the Great Commission we must recognize the broad foundation on which it is built. The missionary enterprise of the church is not a pyramid built upside down with its point on one isolated text in the New Testament out of which we have built a huge structure known as "missions." Rather, the missionary enterprise of the church is a great pyramid built right side up with its base running from Genesis 1 to Revelation 22. All of Scripture forms the foundation for the outreach of the gospel to the whole world. Second, the human dimension of the Great Commission shows that it includes all mankind—every geographic area, all nations; it includes every element, every class of society; it includes every culture and every religion. And finally, the personal responsibility, "*You* are witnesses of these things," covers all Christians. It is your responsibility to carry the gospel to others.

2

On the evening of that day, the first day of the week, the doors being shut where the disciples were, for fear of the Jews, Jesus came and stood among them and said to them, "Peace be with you." When he had said this, he showed them his hands and his side. Then the disciples were glad when they saw the Lord. Jesus said to them again, "Peace be with you. As the Father has sent me, even so I send you." And when he had said this, he breathed on them, and said to them, "Receive the Holy Spirit. If you forgive the sins of any, they are forgiven; if you retain the sins of any, they are retained."

John 20: 19-23

The Son of God Sends His Church

This passage in John 20 makes it plain that we are viewing the same incident we studied in Luke 24. Thus, it is the day of the resurrection when Christ met for the first time with his disciples following the crucifixion.

Luke, with a backward look, emphasizes the continuity from the Old Testament to the mission of Christ and his church. Now John, with a forward look, shows the continuity of the mission of Christ and his church with the future. Johannes Blauw comments, "John . . . indicates the continuity of the sending of the disciples by Jesus; man is, as it were, the arm of God by which He directs His saving acts."[1] The Great Commission, then, is rooted in the eternal purposes of God from the beginning and reaches out through his church to the end of history.

A second fact to note is that while John records the same general incident as that found in Luke, it is almost certainly a different saying. The words are totally different, indicating that Christ gave the Commission twice on the first night in two different ways so they would not miss the point.

Christ knew human psychology. He knew that it is necessary to say something more than once for it to penetrate the minds of most people. He wanted to take no chances that the disciples would miss the point of what he was saying. Therefore, he first gave the basic content to the Great Commission from one angle as recorded by Luke. Later that evening he gave the same thrust but from a totally different angle as recorded by John.

These Are Written That You May Believe

The way John describes how Christ gave the Commission is intimately related to the way he presents Christ throughout the Gospel. John emphasizes Christ as being the Son of God. In fact, John gives a direct statement of his purpose for writing the Gospel: "Now Jesus did many other signs in the presence of the disciples, which are not written in this book; but these are written that you may believe that Jesus is the Christ, the Son of God, and that believing you may have life in his name" (Jn. 20:30-31).

John says, in effect, "In writing this book I have focused on the signs (or miracles) that Jesus did. Now of course Christ performed many miracles, but I have selected a few of them—seven to be exact. I put those signs together so that as you read them and see how they formed a part of the life of Christ, you may believe that he really is Jesus the Messiah, the Son sent from the Father, and that believing you may have eternal life in his name."

Consider for a moment how John organizes the book around those signs. Dr. M. C. Tenney has the finest analysis of these signs that I know of. It is worth quoting here:

> Each of these seven signs revealed some specific characteristic of Jesus' power and person. They are in order:
>
> The changing of Water into Wine 2:1-11
>
> In this first miracle of His ministry, Jesus revealed Him-

self as the master of *quality* by effecting instantaneously the change that the vine produces over a period of months.

The Healing of the Nobleman's Son 4:46-54

By healing the boy who was more than twenty miles distant from Him, Jesus showed Himself the master of *distance* or *space*.

The Healing of the Impotent Man 5:1-9

The longer a disease afflicts a man, the more difficult it is to cure. Jesus, by curing instantly an affliction of thirty-eight years' standing, became the master of *time*.

The Feeding of the Five Thousand 6:1-14

By multiplying the five flat loaves and two small fishes of one boy's lunch into enough to feed five thousand men, besides women and children, Jesus showed Himself to be the master of *quantity*.

The Walking on the Water 6:16-21

This miracle demonstrated His mastery over *natural law*.

The Healing of the Man Born Blind 9:1-2 (41)

The point of this miracle is not so much the fact that Jesus healed a difficult case as that He did so in answer to the question as to why this man should have been so afflicted. Thereby Christ showed that He was master of *misfortune*.

The Raising of Lazarus 11:1-46

This miracle indicated that Jesus incontrovertibly was the master of *death*.

These seven miracles, then, are preeminently *signs* because they point to those aspects of Jesus' ministry in which He demonstrated His transcendent control over the factors of life with which man is unable to cope. . . . Christ's superiority over them as revealed by these events called signs was proof of His deity and a clue to understanding what the writer desired to say about Him.[2]

In addition to the signs there is a secondary element in the organization of the book, namely, the personal interviews. As Jesus reaches people individually, we find more personal interviews in John than in any other Gospel. He sat down alone for a conversation with Nicodemus (Jn. 3). When he came to the city of Samaria, no doubt his heart was moved with compassion as he looked at that great city, just as he was moved by the city of Jerusalem and on other occasions by great crowds. But as he sat down outside Samaria, his heart went out to one person. He concerned himself with the woman by the well, so that she could understand who he was and why he had come (Jn. 4).

Also in John 4 he saw the nobleman and had a brief conversation with him. He conversed personally with the lame man in chapter five. He had quite a talk with the blind man in chapter nine. He went to the home of Mary and Martha in chapter twelve. Mary sat down and listened to him. He also must have included Lazarus in such conversations.

On the day of the resurrection he found Mary Magdalene alone and talked to her (Jn. 20). Luke adds, by the way, that somewhere that day Jesus found Peter and talked alone with him (Lk. 24:34). Later on by the shores of the Sea of Galilee he had another conversation with Peter (Jn. 21).

Do you see what he is doing? As the Son of God who has come to reveal the Father, he demonstrates by individual contact his concern for each person.

Even in the signs themselves there is a primary emphasis on individuals. Of the seven miracles in John, four were performed for the benefit of one person. Of course, other people benefited by seeing it happen. But for the nobleman's son, the lame man at the pool of Bethesda, the blind man and Lazarus the immediate benefit was for them alone.

Another of the signs, walking on the water, was just for the twelve apostles. So out of the seven, only two miracles were performed for the benefit of a large group: the changing of water into wine at Cana and the feeding of the five thousand. It is easy to fall into the habit of seeing vast multitudes in an impersonal way. Now Jesus was moved with compassion by the crowds. But in seeing them he never lost sight of the individuals who made them up.

When I was in college, the whole life of the Dean of Students, Dr. C. C. Brooks, revolved around individuals. He always saw the person as more important than things or rules. When rules had been broken and discipline had to be applied, he always tried to find the best way to salvage the person involved rather than to vindicate a rule. Frequently he would call other students in for counsel to help discover how to reach an obstinate student who was in danger of ruining his own life. I have seen him weep in his office in prayer for individuals whom he was trying to rescue.

As I write these lines Dr. Brooks is over eighty years old but still prays daily for many of the students whom he came to love while he was dean. He has followed with keen interest their activities and has kept in touch to support and encourage them. I could name some outstanding leaders in Christian work today who were salvaged from possible ruin by Dr. Brooks. He saw them as people who needed help rather than as objects who had broken a rule or as statistics describing a crowd.

Christ told the disciples, "As the Father has sent me, even so I send you" (Jn. 20:21). "I came to talk to Nicodemus, to help the Samaritan woman, to heal the blind man, to raise Lazarus. And as my Father sent me to look into the eyes of individuals and love them, so send I you to see every man, every woman as a needy individual for whom I died." As we carry out the Great Commission, we dare not lose sight of that personal touch which Jesus Christ so desperately wants.

One day in Cartagena, Colombia, I was called to help a

young American couple whose two-month-old baby had died mysteriously in the night. Colombia was not their home, so they wished to bury their only child in the United States. The laws of Colombia require burial within twenty-four hours, so they had to move fast. Red tape for getting the child's body out of the country, arranging airplane reservations including space for the coffin and many other details were harrassing them. I spent the day trying to be of what help I could.

During the day another missionary dropped by to offer some comfort. He stayed for a brief while and offered some words of consolation. Somehow what he said reminded me of the pious platitudes of Job's comforters. Finally he said, "Well, just rest on God's strong arms. That's the main thing." And he turned and left. The bereaved young father stood there looking somewhat bewildered. Then we plunged again into the race to get them on the first plane to the United States.

I could not help but wonder how this couple, who did not profess to know Christ, could possibly react to a superficial effort to "evangelize" them at a time of deep grief. They had been treated more as objects than as people. This was not the way of Jesus Christ who came to reach people and who sends us to others as individuals, not as objects.

As the Father Has Sent Me

Now let's look specifically at the Commission. I have already noted that in each one of the Gospels the content of the Commission relates directly to the theme of the book. This comes out classically here. The theme of John is Jesus Christ as the Son of God. Now what did he say in the Commission? As the Son of God he says, "My Father sent me. In the same way I am sending you."

That first verb "to send" is in the aorist tense in Greek while the second verb is in the present tense. The aorist tense normally indicates an action taken once and not repeated; the present tense indicates continued action. "My Father sent me (aorist) with a once-for-all mission. But now I am sending you (present) and will keep on sending you until this job has been done."

In the book of John it is clear that Jesus was sent to reveal the Father. John states this in his prologue: "No one has ever seen God; the only Son, who is in the bosom of the Father, he has made him known" (Jn. 1:18). The Son of God is the one who has made the Father known. No man has ever seen God. But those who have seen the Son have had the Father revealed to them through the Son.

Light, Life and Love

In revealing the Father several great themes come out. Three that are mentioned frequently by John are the themes light, life and love. In John 1, we find an emphasis on light woven intimately together with life.

> In Him was life, and the life was the light of men. The light shines in the darkness, and the darkness has not overcome it. There was a man sent from God, whose name was John. He came for testimony, to bear witness to the light, that all might believe through him. He was not the light, but came to bear witness to the light. The true light that enlightens every man was coming into the world. (Jn. 1:4-9)

Later on Jesus says of himself, "I am the light of the world" (Jn. 8:12). He shines and reveals the truth of God to everyone.

As Jesus also emphasizes life he says, "And this is eternal life, that they know thee the only true God, and Jesus Christ whom thou hast sent" (Jn. 17:3). Again in the prologue, "In him was life, and the life was the light of men" (Jn. 1:4). John 3:16, probably the best-known verse in all the Bible, is so familiar that we sometimes miss the depths of it. But what does it say? "For God so loved the world that he gave his only Son, that whoever believes in him should not perish but have eternal life." This one brief verse includes all the truth of Scripture running from Genesis to Revelation. God, who made the world, loves that world. He loves it so intensely that he has given that which is dearest to his own heart, his only Son, to redeem the world. He desires that all should believe in his Son and thus receive everlasting life with the Father. The entire Old Testament is the preparation for the great act of redemption in Jesus Christ. The entire New Testament is the presentation and explanation of the coming of Jesus Christ and his work of redemption. All of God's activity in the history of redemption is that in his Son men might have everlasting life in glory with the Father.

In another well-known verse Jesus says, "I came that they may have life, and have it abundantly" (Jn. 10:10). This is not only future, eternal life but abundant life right now. Christ is interested in *your* life now. This is part of our message also—that our life is a stewardship from God which is to be cultivated that it might be abundant life now as well as everlasting life later on. "But these are written that you may believe . . . and that believing you may have life in his name" (Jn. 20:31).

In the summer of 1970 I was directing IVCF's first Overseas Training Camp in Costa Rica. We had a group of over forty students from the universities of the United States to give them a one-month exposure to another culture. During the middle period of the camp the students went out by groups into different parts of the country to get first-hand involvement in missionary work.

One afternoon in the capital city of San Jose I received a phone call from the missionary who was heading up one of our teams on the Pacific side of Costa Rica. His voice was tense with emotion as he said to me, "Dave, I hate to tell you this, but we lost one of our boys down here this afternoon."

He went on to explain how they had gone for a picnic on the beach for a little relaxation. While out in the surf, they noticed a strong undertow developing. So he motioned for everyone to come out. All the students came out on the beach except Dale Bowman. They motioned for him to come out, and he indicated that he was coming. A few minutes later they noticed that Dale still hadn't gotten out of the surf. They suddenly realized that he was in trouble, that the undertow had caught him.

Ron Kernaghan, an Inter-Varsity staff member, immediately dove into the surf and went to him. The others ran to find a rope or a boat but were unable to find either. By the time Ron got to him, Dale was weakening considerably. He had been fighting the undertow and the surf. The two of them were carried farther and farther out. Ron hung on to him, but little by little Dale lost all his strength and finally lost consciousness.

For the next forty-five minutes they were swept farther out into the surf while the others on the beach, unable to get a boat or a rope, were frustrated by the fact that there was nothing that they could do. Ron held Dale up, now unconscious, and finally decided that there was no hope at all of getting back to shore. So he resigned himself to die. He determined that he would not leave Dale but rather would drown with him. Eventually he nearly lost consciousness himself.

Suddenly they were hit by a large wave that separated them. Dale was swept one way and Ron the other. Ron made a lunge to get to Dale, but Dale sank beneath the waves, bobbed up once more, and then sank and was never seen again. We never found his body.

Ron has no recollection of what happened after that. The next thing he recalls is being swept up on the beach, staggering out of the surf and collapsing. He spent the next half-hour trying to catch his breath and recuperate.

Upon receiving this word I had to call Dale's parents in the United States. I got them out of bed about midnight to inform them that their son was gone. This was one of the most difficult tasks I had ever performed. When I had finished I jumped in a jeep with missionary Bob Bennett and drove to the coast. We arrived about 3:00 A.M. I spent the next two days with the students who were in a state of shock over this sudden tragedy. I tried to help Ron recuperate both physically and emotionally. He had exerted himself physically far beyond what a human could normally do. Psychologically and spiritually he went through deep struggles wondering why God took Dale and left him.

A week later back at camp he came into my room late one night, and we discussed this at great length. Two years later I asked him, "Ron, what do you think God was trying to teach you in this experience?"

Ron responded, "God has been teaching me the stewardship of life. I am a man who came back from the dead. I had resigned myself to die and was as good as dead. Suddenly I am back in life again. I felt as though I should be beyond the grave with Dale. I used to have dreams of Dale coming to me and saying, 'Why aren't you with me?' "

He realized that God had literally given his life back to him. He said, "I see life in a new way now. I have a greater concept of the stewardship of life as a special gift from God." He was catching the truth that Jesus expressed: "I came that they may have life, and have it abundantly."

There is also emphasis on love in the book of John. "A new commandment I give to you, that you love one another; even as I have loved you, that you also love one another. By this all men will know that you are my disciples, if you have love for one another" (Jn. 13:34-35). If we are not demonstrating the love of Jesus Christ, the love of God the Father, we are not demonstrating true discipleship. Others will not come to know Christ if they don't see love within us. But if they see love in us, that is the first great step toward being attracted to

Christ and through him to a right relationship with God.

Connie Kinch is a missionary but not a pith-helmeted, Bible-toting preacher. His tools are a hammer, a wrench, a saw, a power drill—and a heart full of love. Connie is the maintenance man for the Latin America Mission in Costa Rica. He spends his days repairing vehicles, installing plumbing or wiring, overseeing construction. He has a crew of men working with him, many of whom sign on as non-Christians. But few are the men who remain long with Connie without becoming Christians. The reason is not in his eloquent preaching or flawless Spanish, characteristics of which he has never been accused! But one thing that radiates from Connie is his love for people. In short order he can reprimand a shirker or a lazy worker in Spanish that leaves something to be desired as far as good pronunciation or correct grammar are concerned. But everyone knows that Connie's heart is as big as his monkey wrench.

And he is as unselfish. He will work long hours into the night, if necessary, to finish a job so that a fellow missionary or a Costa Rican can have his car ready for use or his plumbing repaired. He and his wife Esther run open house to anyone in need, in spite of the fact that they have eleven children of their own.

So when Connie talks to someone about Christ, which he does as readily as he installs an electric plug or replaces a gasket, people listen. They listen because they know Connie loves them. I have no idea how many Costa Ricans Connie has led to Christ, but it won't be surprising if in heaven we see him surrounded by far more children in the Lord than many others who have spent their lives in direct preaching. "Many waters cannot quench love," and Connie's love for the Lord and for other people is contagious.

This is the message of John. "As the Father has sent me (to demonstrate love), even so I send you (to do the same)." For

Christ has said, "By this all men will know that you are my disciples, if you have love for one another" (Jn. 13:35). As Christ revealed the Father, he revealed light and life, and he revealed love.

The Work of the Father

Finally, it is made clear in John that Jesus was sent to do the work of the Father. In revealing the Father, he was doing the Father's work. He said, "My Father is working still, and I am working" (Jn. 5:17). "We must work the works of him who sent me, while it is day; night comes, when no one can work" (Jn. 9:4).

In John 6:28 the people said to him, "What must we do, to be doing the works of God?" Notice his answer. They had spoken in the plural, speaking of "works." But Jesus answered in the singular, referring to "the work." "This is the work of God, that you believe in him whom he has sent" (Jn. 6:29). God's great work is that people might believe. The *work*—not the works. It is not as though he has many different things to do. God is attempting to redeem the human race and restore men and women to himself in belief through Jesus Christ. This is *the* work. And that is the heart of everything that we are called to do. "As the Father has sent me (so that men might believe), even so I send you (that men might believe)."

It is not our work to make people believe. That is the work of the Holy Spirit. Our work is to present the facts, the message and the love of Jesus Christ so that they can believe. As we do this we can expect the opposition of Satan who will do everything he can to keep people from believing.

On Christmas Eve of 1959 my wife and I were invited by a neighbor in the city of Cartagena, Colombia, to spend the evening with him and his family. He was a German businessman who had spent most of his life in Latin America. He said,

"We would like to share Christmas Eve with you so that you can see how we Germans celebrate Christmas."

They lived three houses down the street. So after we put the small children to bed, my wife and I went over and spent the rest of Christmas Eve with them. We had a delightful time as they shared their German customs.

Later in the evening he turned and said, "Mr. Howard, I didn't really invite you here just for Christmas Eve. I want to know what it is that you believe. I want to know why you have come to Colombia."

What a wide open opportunity! For the next hour or two I simply explained why we were missionaries and what Jesus Christ had sent us to do. I tried to help him understand the message of the gospel. Finally he said, "Listen, can we study the Bible together sometime?" I said I would be delighted. So periodically over the next six or seven years, we studied the Bible together. He would call up in the evening and say, "Are you free tonight?"

"Yes."

"Well, bring your Bible over and we will study together."

Again and again my friend would come right up to the point of accepting Jesus Christ. Being an intelligent man he understood the gospel clearly and seemed ready to step through into salvation. Then he would step back. His face would tighten up and he would say, "But it is so hard to believe! It is so hard to believe!" He could not take that final step.

I often wondered what was holding him back. It was not that he hadn't heard the whole message for we had discussed it many times. It wasn't that he didn't see Christian love for he spoke of this. Something else was restraining him.

Some years later he told me that his mother had been a spiritist. I am not an authority on spiritism, but I do know that when it exists in a family, this can affect every member of the family. His mother was apparently a worshiper of evil spirits.

If that was true, these same spirits may well have been resisting his becoming a believer. Every time he would step up to the door the restraint would be there. "I cannot believe."

This went on for years, and he never accepted Christ. In December of 1974 I got a letter from him. He was back in Germany. He wrote,

> I wish to thank you for your letter of December 3 and for all good wishes you sent to all our family. We, too, hope that you will have a Happy Christmas. We are especially happy that Jesus Christ entered our house this year and to us all. Therefore, this Christmas season will be of more significance than ever before.

It took fifteen years, but he finally took that step of belief because God broke through. We do the work of Jesus Christ in the world that men might believe through the power of God. For many, belief will be hard. We need patience, grace and understanding to believe that God will work in his own time and way, as he did in the life of my German friend.

Christ was sent to reveal the Father to the world, to bring life and love to us. Christ has commissioned us to do the same through his power. This means first that we must go to those individuals in our immediate situation: our campus, our family, our job, our neighborhood. For some it may mean crossing cultural or geographic or social barriers as we noticed in Luke. It may mean supporting others in prayer or finances as they cross these barriers. We have the clear command from Christ to participate in his outreach to the world.

Receive the Holy Spirit

Before we complete our look into the Gospel of John, we need to discuss two controversial points which occur in a single passage. "And when he had said this, he breathed on them, and said to them, 'Receive the Holy Spirit' " (Jn. 20:22).

There have been numerous debates on the timing of the

disciples receiving the Holy Spirit. Did they receive the Holy Spirit on this occasion, or did they receive the Spirit on the Day of Pentecost? It is somewhat peripheral to my purposes here to enter into a detailed discussion of this question. The important point is that in every case where the Great Commission is given Jesus Christ relates it to a promise of the Spirit or his presence through the Spirit. The Holy Spirit will be with his witnesses so that *he* will carry out the work that he wants to do.

I couldn't make my German friend believe. It was too hard for him. I could not force him through the door of belief. The Holy Spirit finally convinced him. And the Holy Spirit is the one who goes with us. Harry Boer, in *Pentecost and Missions*, has developed a solid biblical case that while the Great Commission forms the foundation for the missionary outreach of the church, it is only the Pentecost experience which allows the Great Commission to be fulfilled. That is the point that Jesus makes here.

While the timing is secondary for our purposes, perhaps a brief word is in order anyway. In Luke 24, on this same night, he said to them, "And behold, I send the promise of my Father upon you; but stay in the city, until you are clothed with power from on high" (Lk. 24:49). That is, Jesus did not clothe them with power that night but indicated that they must remain in Jerusalem until the Spirit came. This breathing on them was in anticipation of what was to come later. He said, "Wait. You are not ready yet. But when you are given power from heaven, then go." Fifty days later on the Day of Pentecost they received the power from on high.

Forgiveness

The second problem in this passage has been debated at length by theologians. Jesus said, "Receive the Holy Spirit. If you forgive the sins of any, they are forgiven; if you retain the sins of any, they are retained" (Jn. 20:22-23). This has been used by some to claim that the apostles received power to forgive sins. *The New Bible Commentary* has a simple yet clear explanation on this: "Although it is not in the power of man to forgive sins, man can pronounce forgiveness on the basis of what God has done in Christ. This is through the agency of the Holy Spirit within him, making him Christ's ambassador."[3] It is not that we have the power to forgive. Only God can do that through Jesus Christ. But we have the authority to declare sins forgiven when the message of Jesus Christ has been given and accepted by those who believe in him. Therefore, our message is one of forgiveness. This is the same truth which he declared in Luke: "that repentance and forgiveness of sins should be preached in his name to all nations, beginning from Jerusalem" (Lk. 24:47).

It is great to see the Holy Spirit at work in bringing people to forgiveness. I have a close friend in Colombia named Eliecer Benavides. If you ever should see Eliecer, you would probably not pick him out as a leader. He is a quiet, rather shy sort of man. Years ago before he became a Christian he worked in a gold mine. Every day he would pilfer a bit of gold, putting it into his shoe or his sock to sneak it out of the mine.

Later he became a Christian. He came to our Bible institute in the town of Sincelejo, Colombia, to prepare for Christian work. One day in class the professor was teaching the story of Zacchaeus. He told how Zacchaeus had apparently cheated people in his tax collecting. When he met Jesus, Zacchaeus said, "I am going to make it right." After class Eliecer told the teacher how he had pilfered gold.

"Now I am a Christian. What am I going to do about it?"

Tom Cherry, the professor, said to him, "Don Eliecer, there is only one thing that you can do. Write to the owner of the gold mine and tell him what you did, offering to make it right."

"But he might put me in prison."

"Yes, he might. That may be the price that you will have to pay. But you make it right."

Eliecer wrote to the owner of the gold mine and told him what he had done. Then he waited for the police to arrive and take him off to prison. Instead, he got a letter from the owner saying, in essence, the following:

"In all my life I have never seen anything like this! A man who was not apprehended in the crime confesses it and wants to make it right. I am so impressed with what you are doing [for Eliecer had told him that he was now studying for the ministry] that I will tell you what I propose. I don't know how much you robbed from me—only you know that. You determine how much you stole. Then go to work and earn that amount of money. Give it to the Bible institute where you are studying, and I will cancel your debt."

So Eliecer dropped out of Bible school, went to work, earned the money and contributed it to the Bible institute. Then he returned and finished his studies.

He had learned the true meaning of forgiveness. He had recognized his sin and had taken steps to rectify the wrong he had committed. He had then been absolved from his guilt because of his confession and because restitution had been made. Since he had learned forgiveness, he became a very effective pastor. He went into the rural areas and began to witness. One of the first men that he led to Jesus Christ was Victor Landero. Victor became God's instrument for a great people movement through a vast area of northern Colombia. And Victor has now led hundreds of people to Jesus Christ. Today there are thousands of believers and scores of congregations in an area where a few years ago there was not one trace of the gospel because Eliecer learned forgiveness.

Later we invited Eliecer to work with us in the Bible Institute. Then one night he was taken in great temptation and fell into sin with a woman. No one knew about it except him and the woman. Yet the next morning he went again to Tom Cherry and confessed his sin.

"Don Tomás, I am through. I have tried and I have failed. This is the end. I will have to leave."

"Yes, I am afraid you will, Don Eliecer," Tom said. "We can't keep you on the staff of the Bible institute right now."

They wept and prayed together and Eliecer left. He went back into the hills and began to farm again. We kept our eye on him. We watched him develop and faithfully walk with the Lord. The time finally came when we said to him, "Eliecer, we want you back."

The first time I saw him after he returned I said, "Don Eliecer, we are so glad that you are back in the ministry with us."

He turned to me with an incredulous look on his face and said, "Don David, I don't know how you could invite me back. You know my weaknesses. You know my failures. How could you possibly invite me back?"

"Because Jesus Christ forgave your sins. He has washed you clean. We want you back because you know his forgiveness."

He continues today. While preparing this book I received a letter from Colombia telling me more about his continued ministry. God is greatly using that man. And what Eliecer experienced is the message that Jesus Christ gives to us as he sends us out. "As the Father has sent me (that I might bring forgiveness to all mankind), even so I send you (to proclaim forgiveness of sins to all the world)."

So we could say to Eliecer, "You are forgiven." Not that we had forgiven his sins. God had. But we could say to him, in all confidence, "Eliecer, you have been cleansed from your sin. God has done his work in you. 'Though your sins be as scarlet, they shall be as snow.' "

3

Now the eleven disciples went to Galilee, to the mountain to which Jesus had directed them. And when they saw him they worshiped him; but some doubted. And Jesus came and said to them, "All authority in heaven and on earth has been given to me. Go therefore and make disciples of all nations, baptizing them in the name of the Father and of the Son and of the Holy Spirit, teaching them to observe all that I have commanded you; and lo, I am with you always, to the close of the age."

Matthew 28:16-20

The King of Kings Proclaims His Dominion

The best known and most often quoted of the Great Commission passages in the New Testament is the one found in Matthew. Johannes Blauw in *The Missionary Nature of the Church* comments:

> Mission was formerly based a little too one-sidedly, and (even) almost exclusively on this "great commission." But the fault lay not in the fact that mission was based on *this* declaration, but in the fact that Matthew 28:18-20 was isolated from the whole Biblical witness.[1]

To Galilee, to the Mountain

I suggested previously that in developing the missionary enterprise of the church we have all too often looked on it as a pyramid built upside down with its point on one or two isolated texts. We must realize that the missionary mandate of the church is actually a pyramid built right side up with its base running from Genesis 1 to Revelation 22. When we have been guilty of taking one or two Great Commission texts and building the whole enterprise around them, we have missed the broad scope of biblical teaching on world outreach. In Luke, for example, Jesus tied the Great Commission to the entire history of salvation from the Old Testament onward.

Let's look at Matthew 28 first in relation to other events following the resurrection. We have seen in Luke and John that the Commission was given on the day of the resurrection when Jesus met with his disciples for the first time after he arose.

In Matthew we find a different situation. Jesus met his disciples in Galilee on a mountain to which he had directed them. Obviously this is a different incident than the one recorded in Luke and John which took place in Jerusalem. Karl Barth in an excellent essay on this passage says: "Significantly, Matthew leads Jesus's history back to the place of its origin (Matt. 4:12-17); to the Galilee of the Gentiles, to the people who walked in darkness and have seen a great light."[2] Barth develops the importance of the fact that Jesus, who began his ministry in Galilee, took his disciples back there. From that same point he gave them the Commission. It is as if Jesus were saying, "As I began my ministry to preach repentance here in the province of Galilee, I am now commanding you to go from here to all nations with the message with which I am entrusting you."

Two Reactions

This meeting with the disciples occurred more than a week after the resurrection. John states that Christ was in Jerusalem, "eight days [after the resurrection, when] his disciples were again in the house, and Thomas was with them . . ." (Jn. 20:26). So it was sometime after that when he was in Galilee. Many commentators believe that this is the incident to which Paul refers in 1 Corinthians 15 when Jesus appeared to over five hundred brethren at once. That may well be true. Matthew does not tell us that nor does Paul state it in Corinthians.

However, it is a good possibility that when Jesus met with more than five hundred brethren at once, he took the opportunity to give the Great Commission to all of them.

Notice the reaction of these people, whether it was just the eleven disciples or whether it was the five hundred brethren. "And when they saw him they worshiped him; but some doubted" (Mt. 28:17). There is a double reaction here. First there is worship which should be the normal reaction in the presence of the King of kings. The word "worship" here (*proskuneo*) is used rather extensively in both Matthew and John, where he is presented as the King of kings and as the Son of God—the object of worship. This particular word is almost absent from Mark and Luke where Jesus is presented as the Servant of the Lord and as the Son of Man. The concept of worship is not emphasized as much. When he is presented as King by Matthew and as Son of God by John, he is seen as worthy of worship.

Worship is reserved for deity or royalty. The old English was originally "worthship," meaning that a person received homage, reverence or honor because he was worthy of it. *Baker's Dictionary of Theology* defines it, "The worthiness of an individual to receive special honor in accordance with that worth."[3]

Such honor was reserved for kings. Jesus, as the King of kings, was worthy of such honor, and this was rendered to him by the disciples who saw him after the resurrection. They now recognized more fully than ever before that the Son of God had established his sovereignty as the King over all of heaven and earth by his defeat of the power of death.

These disciples had walked, talked, eaten, worked and rested with this man. They had seen him become tired and hungry, sad and joyful, angry and loving, condemning and forgiving. They knew he was a human being just as they were. They knew he was the son of a carpenter. They were acquainted with his brothers and his mother, and possibly with Joseph the carpenter also. As John testifies in 1 John 1:1 they had looked upon him with their eyes, heard him speak with their ears and touched him with their hands. Yet now these same men were worshiping him! What an awesome change! This man who had been born in a lowly stable and had walked the dusty roads of Judea, who had been spit upon and rejected by his own people, crucified in the most ignominious way possible, and buried in a borrowed tomb, was now being worshiped as the King of kings and the Son of God!

The word that Matthew uses for "doubt" (*distadzo*) should also be noted. The only other time it appears in the New Testament is in the story of Peter walking on the water (Mt. 14: 22-33). When he saw the winds and waves, he was afraid and he doubted. That is, he became perplexed and confused. It is not a word which implies unbelief as much as another Greek word also translated "doubt." Rather it implies confusion. The disciples are not quite sure what is going on here. It is not so much that they didn't believe that this was Jesus the Christ, the Son of God. Rather, they were perplexed. They wavered. Karl Barth comments,

> Revelation always has a *terminus a quo* and a *terminus ad quem*. Veiled, it arouses doubt; unveiled, it commands worship. All of us waver again and again between the two. Rieger is therefore right when he says that this sentence was included "as a reminder that faith requires struggle. Don't be surprised if your belief is a continuous conquest of unbelief."[4]

There is nothing wrong with doubt in the proper sense of the word. I have been greatly helped in studying the book of Job. One thing that stands out throughout the book is that the man who presents the greatest doubts is Job himself. His three friends seem to have no doubts about anything. They have the answers. Everything is categorized. The issues are clear to them. There are no problems. Yet after Job has poured out great doubts and come very close to denying his faith in the Lord, God speaks at the end of that book to the three friends: "You have not spoken of me what is right, as my servant Job has" (Job 42:7). God seemed more pleased with the honest expressions of doubt, confusion, perplexity and wavering that came truthfully from Job's full heart than he was with the friends' attempt to put it all together with easy answers. God commends Job whereas he condemns the three friends.

I once heard Norman Grubb, that great elder statesman of missions and delightful Christian gentleman, give his personal testimony. He was telling a group of Inter-Varsity leaders of his student days at Cambridge University immediately after World War 1. He was among those whom God used in establishing the Inter-Varsity movement in England. As he went to the university after the war, he went through a period of perplexity and doubt. He told about the struggles in his own faith—a man who today stands in such a towering position of faith that it is hard to believe that he ever had any doubts. He said, with a twinkle in his eye, "You know, you have to have a good dose of doubt if you are going to have a good dose of faith." How true! Those who seem strongest in faith are often those who at one period or another in their life have been led through confusion and doubt. Tennyson caught this when he wrote, "There lives more faith in honest doubt, believe me, than in half the creeds."[5]

My brother Phil is an example of this. In the late forties he was preparing to go to the mission field. Then suddenly, in ways that were hard to explain, Phil was cast into a period of depression and doubt. For many months, which extended into years, he struggled in deep darkness with questions and doubts about the justice of God. There may have been times when he even questioned God's existence. This confusion held him up from getting to the mission field for several years.

At last, very slowly and with no great dramatic move, God graciously pulled him out of this slough of despondency and restored to him the joy of his salvation.

Phil then went up to the frozen expanses of the Northwest Territories of Canada. He settled in an area where the gospel had never before penetrated. He went to a remote Indian tribe near the shores of the Great Slave Lake and began to hack out an existence there. He built a log cabin, traveling by dog sled in the winter and canoe in the summer. During the winter he had to chop holes in the ice every day to get his water. He heated his cabin with logs sawed by hand.

Slowly he began to learn their language and reduce it to writing. Little by little he began to translate the Scriptures and to witness to these Indians. Phil lived in one little Indian village called Nahanni for fourteen years attempting to lead these Indians to Jesus Christ without seeing one convert!

Some strategists today might take the viewpoint that when you encounter a resistant people like that, you should shake the dust off your feet and move to a receptive area. Yet Phil felt called by God to stay there and keep witnessing until God, in his own time, should break through. But how could he endure that? How could he stay in one village, in the face of opposition, witnessing to the same limited group of Indians, some of whom wanted nothing to do with him, for fourteen years and still see no results? The reason is that Phil is a man of faith because he went through periods of deep doubt. God brought him through those periods and made him strong in faith because he understands what it is to struggle with doubt.

So when we find doubts in our own life or in the lives of people to whom we minister, let's not be too negative. In the midst of their doubts Jesus came with a great word for them.

Worship and doubt are not nearly so far apart from each other as one might expect, as Karl Barth suggests. If we recognize Jesus as the King of kings, then worship becomes spontaneous. We cannot see him as the Lord of all the universe without responding in worship. Having done that we are in no position to question nor to disobey his command. Therefore, worship is basic to our response to the Great Commission. Worship and obedience go hand in hand.

Doubt may also form an integral part of our understanding of his command. If we have gone through some doubts (as most believers have at one time or another), we can empathize better with those whom we evangelize. And, having conquered our doubts, we are stronger than before in our response to the authority of the King.

Recently our youngest son broke a bone in his hand in a high school wrestling match. As the doctor showed us the X rays, he kindly described the healing process that would take place. He explained how the body would build up a new layer of calcium in the crack, actually causing a lump for a while because there would be more calcium than needed to fill the crack. He then said that the bone would be stronger than before because of the extra deposit.

So it is with doubt. A temporary break can produce greater strength. When a follower of Jesus Christ has suffered through his doubts, he will come forth stronger. The Apostle Thomas is seldom mentioned without the adjective "doubting" attached to his name. "Doubting Thomas" is a familiar phrase used to describe him and anyone during the last two thousand years who has had any doubts. Yet the tradition of the early church tells us that Thomas traveled as far as India in response to the Great Commission. The Mar Thoma Church of India claims that it is a direct spiritual descendant of that great apostle. If this be true, and it very well could be, then Thomas probably traveled farther with the gospel message than any of the other twelve apostles. Could it be that, having passed through his doubts, he came out stronger and better able to undertake the rigors of such outreach?

Jesus Christ . . . Son of Abraham

Having seen where Matthew 28:16-20 fits with the other accounts, let's see where it fits within the book itself. We have been noticing that the Great Commission relates directly to the theme of the Gospel in which it appears. Matthew has deep roots in the Old Testament. At least eight times a key phrase appears in Matthew relating that Jesus did or said certain things "that it might be fulfilled which was spoken by the prophets." Matthew then gives the appropriate quote from the Old Testament. This shows Matthew's intention to demonstrate to the Jews that Jesus was the promised Messiah.

The genealogy in Matthew indicates immediately that his main audience was the Jews. It begins with Abraham. In Luke, when Jesus is presented as the Son of Man, the genealogy starts with Adam. But Matthew, writing to the Jews, presents Jesus as the Son of Abraham.

Jesus Christ . . . Son of David

Matthew also emphasizes the kingship of Jesus Christ. This comes out in the first verse of the Gospel: "The book of the genealogy of Jesus Christ, the son of David, the son of Abraham" (Mt. 1:1). Matthew traces Christ through the kingly line as the Son of David. "I am writing a book," Matthew says, "about a King, the son of David. This is the King of the Jews who was promised." In chapter two we read, "Where is he who has been born king of the Jews? For we have seen his star in the East . . . (Mt. 2:2). In describing the triumphal entry into Jerusalem, Matthew quotes Zechariah 9:9, "Your king is coming to you . . ." (Mt. 21:5). In the eschatological discourse in chapters twenty-four and twenty-five, Christ is also presented as the King who will come in power and great glory.

Although it is a Gospel emphasizing primarily the Jewish

ancestry of Jesus Christ and his relationship to the Old Testament, Matthew does not forget the Gentiles. *The New Bible Handbook* comments:

> If chapter i. presents Jesus as the heir to Jewish hopes, chapter ii. shows Him as the fulfilment of Gentile aspirations; the wise men from the East come to do Him homage in the spirit of the prophecy, "Gentiles shall come to thy light, and kings to the brightness of thy rising." (Is. lx.3) . . . The early introduction of the Gentiles in chapter ii. indicates that this Gospel is not exclusively Jewish in its sympathies, and this is borne out by the closing sentence of Mt., which records the risen Lord's commission to His disciples to go and make disciples *of all the nations.* (xxviii.19.)[6]

That is important. When in the final verses of this Gospel Jesus Christ spoke about all nations, the groundwork had already been laid throughout the book. There is an emphasis on the Gentiles. There is an emphasis on all nations. Chapter four speaks of "Galilee of the Gentiles." In chapter eight Jesus healed the servant of the centurion, a Gentile. "He shall proclaim justice to the Gentiles" is quoted from Isaiah 42 in chapter twelve of Matthew. Thus, while it is a Gospel directed primarily to the Jews, the Gentiles are not neglected.

It is also a Gospel of teaching. This is important to notice since in this Great Commission passage Jesus emphasizes the need to teach in the making of disciples.

The Gospel of Matthew is developed around five great discourses. The Sermon on the Mount gives ethical teaching in chapters five to seven. In chapter ten the teaching on mission is given when Jesus charges the twelve and sends them out. The parables of the kingdom are found in chapter thirteen. The relationships within the kingdom—the ecclesiastical teachings—are in chapter eighteen. Then in chapters twenty-four and twenty-five we read the great eschatological discourse with teachings about the end times. When Jesus told his disciples to teach and make disciples of all nations, he had already given the example.

"All Authority Has Been Given to Me"

We are now prepared to ask specifically, "How does the King speak to the disciples as he commissions them?" "Jesus came and said to them, 'All authority in heaven and on earth has been given to me' " (Mt. 28:18). The first part of this Commission is the declaration of authority. As the King, he speaks of his absolute rule. Where did it come from? It was given to him by God.

Ephesians 1 tells how God highly exalted him above all principalities and powers. Philippians 2 gives the reason for this.

> And being found in human form he humbled himself and became obedient unto death, even death on a cross. Therefore God has highly exalted him and bestowed on him the name which is above every name, that at the name of Jesus every knee should bow, in heaven and on earth and under the earth, and every tongue confess that Jesus Christ is Lord, to the glory of God the Father. (Phil. 2:8-11)

The exaltation of Jesus Christ is based on his obedience in death and his victory over death in resurrection. Because of this, he has absolute authority.

The Greek word for "authority," *exousia*, has a specific significance. Arndt and Gingrich give a number of definitions. But their first is, "Freedom of choice, right to act, decide, or dispose of one's property as one wishes."[7] Thus, Jesus Christ has the right to dispose of his property as he wishes. Christ is saying, "I have all authority in heaven and in earth. Everything is mine. Therefore, I have a right to do as I wish with what is mine." His absolute authority extends, first of all, to heaven.

John Stott, in a series of addresses on the Great Commission given in Berlin at the World Congress on Evangelism in 1966, commented on this passage:

> It signifies that Jesus Christ has supreme authority in those "heavenly places" . . . in which evil "principalities and powers" still operate and wage war. . . . The authority of Jesus Christ extends over all creatures, whether human or superhuman, over the Church, over the nations, over the Devil and all his works.[8]

When we are sent by God to preach the message of good news, we will come up against satanic opposition. So we need the assurance of the authority that Christ has over all powers.

In the history of the Christian church it has always been true that when the gospel enters an area for the first time there will be satanic opposition. Christians can count on that. In my years in Colombia we were privileged to work from time to time in areas where the gospel was just beginning to penetrate. Invariably, when it began to take root, there would be satanic opposition.

In North America the gospel has been a leavening influence from the beginning of our country. Nevertheless, our country has sold itself to all forms of evil in recent years. This has again opened the way for an upsurge of satanic opposition to the spread of the gospel. One of the major trends among students in recent years has been intense interest in the occult. I have been asked to speak on witchcraft so often that I have finally refused to do so for my own spiritual good. I have never spoken on that topic without having had a real struggle in my own heart.

One night at the University of Wisconsin I did discuss witchcraft. A large number of students showed up. After the meeting many stayed to ask questions. After most of these had left one fellow came up to me with his fiancée. I could see that he was very agitated and nervous.

He said, "Sir, I have one question."

I said, "What is it?"

"Can a man who has sold himself to Satan—body, soul and spirit—ever be delivered?"

He stood there trembling as he spoke. He did not identify the person about whom he was speaking. But as I asked him a few questions it became obvious that he was talking about himself. One of the Christian students standing nearby saw the seriousness of this and suggested that this fellow and I go off in a room together and talk. But I also asked one of the students to come with me because I never want to face a situation like that without the backing of another Christian. This is not a matter to be played with lightly. We were up against evils and principalities and powers, and we dared not stand against them alone. The Christian fellow came with me and prayed while a number of Inter-Varsity students prayed in another room.

For the next hour and a half the young man opened up and told me things such as I had never heard before. As part of a satanic worship group he had literally sold himself to Satan. He had sliced his finger, filled a vial with blood and passed it around among the other witches with whom he was working. They all drank it as a sacrifice to Satan. He told me, "I now belong to Satan. They tell me that I can never be delivered. They have warned me that if I told the things that I am telling you tonight I will be killed." He described the manner in which he would be killed by these satanic forces. He told me how Satan appeared to him regularly, how he worshiped Satan and prayed to Lucifer every night.

I realized we were in a terrible struggle that night. I felt the need then, more than ever before, of the authority of Jesus Christ. I would have been utterly paralyzed had it not been for the fact that I *knew* Jesus Christ had said, "All authority is given unto me in heaven as well as on earth and I am giving you this authority."

Finally he turned to me and said, "Is there any deliverance for me?"

I said, "There is only one thing more powerful than the blood that you have sacrificed to Satan. That is the blood of Jesus Christ that can cleanse you from all sin."

"Can you do that for me?"

"No, you yourself have to turn to Jesus Christ, and he will cleanse you."

"How can I do it?"

I explained the principles of the gospel. "You have prayed to Lucifer. You have to pray to Jesus Christ tonight. I will pray for you first, then I want you to pray." The minute I started to pray he toppled to the floor and began to cry out in pain. He grabbed himself and went through awful wretchings, the type of thing described in Mark when Jesus cast out demons.

Although I had a terrible human fear, at the same time I had a sense of the power of Jesus Christ who had said, "All authority is given to me." I laid my hands on him and claimed deliverance through the authority of Jesus Christ. He calmed down, sat back up in his chair and began to pray. He poured out his heart in worship to God in one of the most beautiful prayers I have ever heard. When he finished he turned with a big smile on his face and said, "Wow! This is real! This has really happened!"

Then I turned to his fiancée, who had accompanied us and had been listening to all of this. I asked about her relationship to God. She replied that she was not sure what it was. After a brief explanation of the gospel, she too indicated her desire to receive Jesus Christ and did so in prayer.

Later that year this young couple asked me to perform their wedding. It was a small private wedding but one of the most significant I had ever performed. It was a solemn privilege to join in marriage two people who had experienced in their lives the delivering power of God. While the young lady had not herself been involved in satanism, she had seen its devastating effects in her fiancé's life and so joined him in commitment to Jesus Christ.

Nearly two years later they came to see me. He was in the military service and was on his way to Germany. He came to thank me again that he had now come into deliverance and knew Jesus Christ. He said, "I believe God has a mission for me now in Germany. I am looking forward to going so I can serve God there."

What is the result of this authority in Christ's command? We are to go and make disciples of all nations. John Stott puts it this way: "The fundamental basis of all Christian missionary enterprise is the universal authority of Jesus Christ."[9]

Make Disciples of All Nations

What, then, is Christ's message to us? In Matthew's Great Commission passage there is only one command in the original text along with several participles. The word *go*, although rendered in most English translations as an imperative, is actually a participle. It could be translated *as you go*. The imperative is *make disciples.* It isn't a question of whether or not we are to go. This is assumed. But, as we go, we are to make disciples.

It was delightful to watch my friends in Colombia who were new Christians. I previously mentioned Victor Landero and how he was led to Jesus Christ by Eliecer. When he became a Christian, he was making his living partly by farming. But he was also living partly by operating a brothel where he had several prostitutes working for him. He lived with three women at the same time—one in his brothel, one on his farm and one in the next village up the road. He wasn't married to any of them.

When he became a Christian, he immediately began to witness to others. He led his whole family to the Lord—eight brothers and sisters as well as his father and mother. He led most of those in his village to Christ. Soon they had a little church going. They built a thatched roofed chapel and a rustic pulpit. They had no missionaries or pastors to teach them, so Victor did the teaching. He was totally uneducated, having never been to first grade, as was the case with many of my Colombian friends. He had learned how to read but that was the extent of his education. Yet he would saturate himself in the Scriptures.

One day Victor realized that he had so thoroughly evangelized around his farm that almost everyone in the area had heard the gospel. He understood that other people ought to hear this too. So he called his brothers together with whom he jointly owned the farm.

"I've got an idea," he said. "There are people up the San Pedro River that never heard the gospel. We have a happy fellowship here. We have a church going. I think it would be a good idea if you bought out my share of the farm. I'll take that money, go up the San Pedro River and buy a plot of ground to start farming there. I can witness there and you can keep on going with the church here." His brothers agreed. Victor bought a plot of ground, hacked out the jungle and started to farm. He also began to witness in that area. Soon people were coming to Christ.

He had never heard a message on the Great Commission. To him the question of going was simply an assumed responsibility. Now that his family and friends had heard the gospel he had to keep going.

He came to the conclusion that one day out of the week, Sunday, belonged to God. He prayed, "Now, God, I'd like to give more time to witnessing for you. One day is yours. There are six days left in the week. I'll make a fifty-fifty deal with you. I'll divide those six days and spend three of them farming if you will help me keep my farm up in three days of work. I'll spend the other three days going out witnessing."

When he told me about this I asked, "How did it work, Victor?"

He said, "It worked so well that I found that I could keep my farm going with two days of work, and I had four days left to witness." It wasn't that he had to be commanded to go. He simply was going. And he got other people moving. He organized the men in church and sent them out on weekends. I watched him at a Thursday evening prayer meeting when he organized the coming weekend's activities.

He said, "Now who will go to such and such a village this weekend?" One man would raise his hand. "Well, somebody else has to go with you." Victor had discovered in the Scriptures that when Jesus sent out his disciples he sent them two by two. So Victor always sent two men as they went out to witness.

As I was preparing this book I received a letter from Victor's brother, Gregorio, a speaker at the Urbana 73 Missionary Convention. He urged me to return to Colombia for a visit and then went on to say, "When you come we want to go visit Victor. But it won't be easy to get to him now. Victor has moved out among the Catío Indians farther back in the jungle. If you come you must allow time so that we can get back where the Indians are."

The command to "make disciples" means that we must help people not only to confess Jesus Christ but develop a life of true discipleship. For Victor obedience to the Great Commission required him to keep moving. Having evangelized as thoroughly as possible in his own area, he felt compelled to move out to the next unevangelized area. As Christians we are to be sensitive to God's leading in seeking to reach those who do not know him. If this means to keep moving elsewhere, we must obey. If it means to become a more effective witness and disciple where we are, we must obey.

The World Is Our Parish

Throughout the Gospel of Matthew Jesus emphasizes that the world is our parish. In his parable of the tares in chapter thirteen he says that "the field is the world." In the parable of the marriage feast in chapter twenty-two the king sends his servants out into the highways and byways to bring everyone in. No one is to be excluded from the feast.

In the discourse on the last times, Jesus makes the great statement, "This gospel of the kingdom will be preached throughout the whole world, as a testimony to all nations; and then the end will come" (Mt. 24:14). Johannes Blauw makes a significant point in commenting on this: "One will have to pass Israel's boundaries consciously and intentionally to be able to fulfill the order."[10] That is, there must be a conscious crossing of geographic frontiers. I am often asked, "Why do you emphasize foreign missions so much?" The simple reason is that if the gospel is to go to all nations, the only way this will be accomplished is by crossing geographic as well as cultural borders. That is foreign missions. We may react against the concept of "foreign missions," but we cannot avoid the implications of Matthew 28.

Karl Barth says, "Already the relationship to verse 18 and its parallels rules out any limitation of Jesus' dominion. How could he, to whom all power is given, have ever intended founding a pious little Jewish club?"[11] He wasn't founding a pious little Jewish club. He was founding a group of men who would reach to all nations.

If the Great Commission is to be fulfilled, some of us will have to cross geographic frontiers. Missiologists tell us that there are nearly three billion people in the world today who have no knowledge of Jesus Christ. Most of them are outside of North America. If North American Christians are to be obedient, how can we avoid the possibility that some of us must go to other areas where the gospel has not yet been given? This is true, of course, for Christians from other parts of the world as well. No part of the body of Christ can avoid its responsibility to carry the gospel to those who do not have it. And for some this requires crossing borders.

This does not mean that every Christian must go to another area of the world. Such a contention would be unbiblical and foolish. But it does mean that every Christian must be concerned for the world and actively involved in helping to get the gospel to those who do not have it.

In discussing Luke's Gospel we also saw this will require crossing cultural borders. Within our own geographic area we have a wide variety of cultures which divide us. Across these frontiers are many people who have no knowledge of salvation. Our obedience to God will involve some in crossing these borders as well.

This will mean reaching out in love and practical concern for those of different ethnic and racial backgrounds who may be located in our same geographical area. It will mean concern of white people for black friends, of black brothers for Chinese friends, of Chinese people for Chicano neighbors, of Chicano friends for American Indians, of Christians for Jewish people, of middle-class Americans for Polish immigrants, of Polish Christians for Puerto Rican neighbors. The possible combinations are endless, but the responsibility of the church of Jesus Christ for the world is unchangeable.

What about the method? This is given in two participles—baptizing and teaching. Baptism is administered when men and women make a public recognition of their relationship to the body of Christ. Through baptism, as a recognition of what has happened to them spiritually, there is a public declaration of faith. In our land baptism can be administered freely and there is no great problem. This is not true everywhere today.

In 1974 I attended the International Congress on World

Evangelization in Lausanne, Switzerland. I had the privilege of leading a workshop entitled, "Witnessing Under Hostile Governments." Most of the people who attended that workshop were from lands where they live and witness under adverse conditions. There were two Russians, three Hungarians, a Romanian, men from Poland and Yugoslavia, and one from Nepal, among others.

Some were very cautious about how they spoke. The Hungarians, for example, seemed to be convinced that the Congress was infiltrated with spies and that anything they said could be held against them when they returned to Hungary. They were frightened and thus cautious.

The man from Nepal said nothing the first two days. Finally, on the third day I said to him, "Brother, we don't want to embarrass you, and you don't have to speak if you don't care to. But if you would like to share anything about your experiences in Nepal, we would love to hear from you."

He spoke up with a big smile on his face and said, "Yes, I will be glad to share. Let me tell you what it means to be a Christian in Nepal. We have a saying there that the birth certificate of a Christian is one year in jail. The minute you become a Christian you can count on spending the next year behind bars. Then if you take the step of baptism, where you outwardly identify yourself with the Christian church, you will probably spend the next six years in jail. So our baptismal certificate is a six-year jail sentence."

One of the Russians had spent time in the slave labor camps of northern Siberia, which we read about in *The Gulag Archipelago*, for being baptized and standing up for his faith.

Baptism is an outward symbol of the regeneration that takes place through faith in Jesus Christ. Such a step will be costly for Christians in Nepal, Russia and elsewhere. Yet it is part of the cost of discipleship. Discipleship requires a total commitment to Christ. That commitment will be demonstrated in baptism, as confession is made of faith in him. Thus, when Jesus told his followers to "make disciples," he included baptism as part of that process.

Jesus then says to the disciples that they are to teach all things which they had observed and which he had commanded—the whole counsel of God. This includes all the Old Testament and all the New Testament.

Finally comes the great promise, "Lo, I am with you always, to the close of the age" (Mt. 28:20). There is no time that he will not be with us. It is a great thing to know and to experience that truth.

I recall vividly the first time I went to an area in Colombia where there was demon activity. I had never been, to my knowledge, in the presence of a demon-possessed person. I did not know how I would react when I came face to face with such a person.

Travel to that area was a three-day trip requiring a long day by jeep, another by canoe and another half day on foot. On the third day, before heading off into the jungles on foot, apprehensive about what I would face, I opened my Bible. The Lord wonderfully gave me that verse in Isaiah, "For the Lord God helps me; therefore I have not been confounded; therefore I have set my face like a flint, and I know that I shall not be put to shame" (Is. 50:7). God said to me, "That is my word for you today. You are going into demon-possessed areas, but I will be with you even unto the end of the age. I will be with you there in that area." I went with a lightness in my heart. I did come in contact with demon-possessed people, and I sensed the presence and the power of the Lord who had said, "Lo, I am with you always, to the close of the age."

Notice also the comprehensive use of the word *all* in the Great Commission in Matthew.

All authority—there is no power that is left out.

All nations—there is no person that is left out.

All things—there is no precept that is left out.
All times—there is no period that is left out.
This is the way he sends us.

What about us today? The King of kings is the one who says, "All authority is mine and, therefore, I am sending you." On that basis we have an obligation to obey and a right to go to every nation with the gospel.

The command given in Matthew is to "make disciples of all nations." This makes the idea of going both implicit and imperative. How can we make disciples of all nations unless we go to all nations? We are under the authority of Christ; therefore, we go so we can fulfill the command to make disciples.

To fulfill this command, many Christians have gone to extreme measures such as smuggling Bibles into closed lands. There are strong differences of opinion today about the ethics of doing this. I am not in a position to debate the merits of this practice because I have not lived in that kind of place. It is only fair to say that we who have not suffered under such restrictions dare not judge people on either side of that argument.

Brother Andrew has written a book called *The Ethics of Smuggling.* I commend it as a book worth studying. I do not agree with everything Brother Andrew says. I am not sure that he builds his case adequately in some points. But he makes a biblical case for the fact that we have the *right* to give the gospel to every country in the world. He says, in effect, "No government has the right to tell a Christian that he cannot obey the command of his King." We may debate back and forth this particular issue of Bible smuggling, but we cannot avoid our responsibility, based on Christ's authority, to give his Word to all nations.

There is no way around the Great Commission for a Christian. It is an imperative. This does not mean that every Christian should, therefore, cross geographic boundaries. That isn't the point. The point is that no Christian can ignore his duty of discipling the nations.

Finally, we have the confidence for doing so. "Lo I am with you always. . . ."

"We go" in faith, our own great weakness feeling,
 And needing more each day Thy grace to know:
Yet from our hearts a song of triumph pealing;
 "We rest on Thee, and in Thy name we go."

4

Now when he rose early on the first day of the week, he appeared first to Mary Magdalene, from whom he had cast out seven demons. She went and told those who had been with him, as they mourned and wept. But when they heard that he was alive and had been seen by her, they would not believe it.

After this he appeared in another form to two of them, as they were walking into the country. And they went back and told the rest, but they did not believe them.

Afterward he appeared to the eleven themselves as they sat at table; and he upbraided them for their unbelief and hardness of heart, because they had not believed those who saw him after he had risen. And he said to them, "Go into all the world and preach the gospel to the whole creation. He who believes and is baptized will be saved; but he who does not believe will be condemned. And these signs will accompany those who believe: in my name they will cast out demons; they will speak in new tongues; they will pick up serpents, and if they drink any deadly thing, it will not hurt them; they will lay their hands on the sick and they will recover."

So then the Lord Jesus, after he had spoken to them, was taken up into heaven, and sat down at the right hand of God. And they went forth and preached everywhere, while the Lord worked with them and confirmed the message by the signs that attended it. Amen.

Mark 16:9-20

The Servant of the Lord Defines Our Ministry

We turn now to the most controversial of the Great Commission passages, that found in Mark 16. The most ancient manuscripts of Mark available to us today do not include 16: 9-20. There are various theories which scholars have put forth to explain what happened at the end of that Gospel.

One theory, propounded by R. H. Lightfoot in his *Gospel of Mark*, is that Mark intended to end with verse eight and that the longer ending was added later by someone else. Another theory is that the original ending of Mark has been lost, and what we now have in our text is a later attempt to reconstruct what Mark actually said. Then there are those scholars who defend the text as we have it today in available manuscripts. Principal among these is Dean J. W. Burgon in his elaborate defense of the concluding section of Mark's Gospel entitled *The Last Twelve Verses of the Gospel According to St. Mark* published in 1871. I have been informed by New Testament scholars that this work is recently being revived and restudied in the field of New Testament scholarship. Dr. Samuel Zwemer also includes an eloquent defense of these verses in his classical work on the Great Commission entitled *Into All the World* published in 1943.

Personally, I find it hard to believe that Mark intended to end with 16:8. If he did, he certainly left the Gospel in an unfinished state. It seems more probable that he continued to a more suitable ending. Whether the actual text that we have now is that which Mark originally wrote or is a reconstruction of it, Mark quite probably added more beyond verse eight.

There is a further theological point which should be mentioned here. In all the other Gospels, the Great Commission is an integral part of the message. We find the story of the life and ministry of Jesus Christ, his death and his resurrection followed by the giving of the Great Commission. These basic elements cannot be removed without emasculating the gospel message.

In other words, if the message of the life, death and resurrection of Jesus Christ does not go to all the world, then the work of Jesus Christ is in vain. For this reason, it is indispensable that the Great Commission be included as an essential part of every Gospel. Without it, the gospel is incomplete. Therefore, while fully recognizing the textual variations and the problems involved, I leave the solution to competent scholars and choose to accept the longer ending of Mark as containing valid material about Jesus Christ and the Commission to his church.

Mark does not make clear to us when this incident took place. Many commentators place it along with Luke and John as being on the day of the resurrection. This is quite possible although not certain. It is also conceivable that Mark could be recording the same incident which Matthew gives us although this seems less likely. A third possibility is that Mark is recording another incident not given in any of the other three Gospels. However, because Mark is silent on the timing of this, we can make no special point of the chronological sequence here.

The Son Came to Serve

Jesus is presented by Mark as the Servant of the Lord. This theme runs clearly throughout the Gospel in a number of different ways.

First, there is no genealogy. Matthew, as we have seen, traces Jesus to Abraham. Luke, who presents Jesus as the Son of Man, traces him to Adam. Yet a genealogy in biblical times was not important for a servant. Clearly it was important for a king and, therefore, Matthew could not exclude it. But in presenting Christ as a servant, a genealogy was not indispensable.

Second, there is a predominance of deeds over teaching. Mark emphasizes consistently what Jesus *did* rather than what he *taught*. It is the Gospel which tells us the story of a man in action on behalf of other people.

Third, miracles form an important part of the Gospel. Tenney points out, "For its size, Mark gives more space to the miracles than does any other Gospel, for it records 18 out of a possible 35. . . . Plainly Mark was more interested in deeds than in speculation."[1] Miracles were always used to serve other people and to glorify God. If Jesus were a true servant—serving both man and God—then the use of miracles was consistent with this servanthood.

Fourth, Mark's use of the two Greek words *euthus* and *eutheos*, meaning "immediately," is indicative of the activist nature of the Gospel. These words are used forty-two times, more than in all the rest of the New Testament put together. Thus the movement throughout the Gospel is rapid. Jesus was "immediately" moving from one action to another.

Fifth, it is interesting that the disciple who was more of an activist than any other was Peter. He was always on the move, always doing or saying something. We are told by ancient history that Mark was considered the "interpreter of Peter." Although we do not read of Peter and Mark being together in the New Testament, this ancient tradition is highly probable. Peter refers to him as "my son Mark" (1 Pet. 5:13). If Peter actually took Mark under his wing and Mark became his interpreter, it is understandable that there was an activist emphasis. This tradition comes from the famous quote in Eusebius' *Ecclesiastical History* (A.D. 326) in which he quotes Papias (c. A.D. 140) as saying:

> And John the presbyter also said this, Mark being the interpreter of Peter, whatsoever he recorded he wrote with great accuracy, but not however, in the order in which it was spoken or done by our Lord, but as before said, he was in company with Peter, who gave him such instruction as was necessary, but not to give a history of our Lord's discourse: wherefore Mark has not erred in any thing, by writing some things as he has recorded them; for he was carefully attentive to one thing, not to pass by any thing he had heard, or to state any thing falsely in these accounts.[2]

Sixth, the Old Testament book which presents the Messiah as the Servant of Jehovah more than any other is Isaiah. It is no accident that Mark begins his Gospel with a quote from Isaiah. Having introduced the Gospel in verse one by saying, "The beginning of the Gospel of Jesus Christ, the Son of God," Mark immediately quotes Isaiah: "As it is written in Isaiah the prophet, 'Behold, I send my messenger before thy face, who shall prepare thy way; the voice of one crying in the wilderness: Prepare the way of the Lord, make his paths straight" (Mk. 1:2-3).

Last, a key verse to the Gospel of Mark is 10:45: "For the Son of man also came not to be served but to serve, and to give his life as a ransom for many." Jesus made this statement when James and John, the sons of Zebedee, asked permission to sit, one at his right hand and one at his left, in glory. Jesus pointed out that service, rather than position, is what counts in God's sight. He said, "You know that those who are supposed to rule over the Gentiles lord it over them, and their great men exercise authority over them. But it shall not be so among you; but whoever would be great among you must be your servant, and whoever would be first among you must be slave of all" (Mk. 10:42-44).

Thus, with an emphasis on deeds and miracles, on immediacy of action, and on servanthood, Mark presents Christ as the Servant of the Lord reaching out in concern to people. With this in mind it is surprising to see the mood that prevailed among the disciples when Christ gave them the Great Commission in Mark.

The Gospel to the Whole Creation

Mark presents the Great Commission in an atmosphere of unbelief. Three times in this brief paragraph unbelief is referred to. When Mary Magdalene returned from the tomb and told the others who had been with him that Jesus was alive, "they would not believe it" (Mk. 16:11). Later that day when he appeared to two of them as they were walking in the country (unquestionably the two men on the road to Emmaus referred to by Luke) these men went back and told the rest, "but they did not believe them" (Mk. 16:13). Afterward, Jesus himself appeared to the eleven as they sat at a table "and he upbraided them for their unbelief and hardness of heart, because they had not believed those who saw him after he had risen" (Mk. 16:14).

It is in this context of unbelief that the content of the gospel is mentioned. What was it that they did not believe? They refused to believe the *resurrection*, the touchstone of the gospel. G. Campbell Morgan says,

> What then is "the Gospel"? It is the good news that the Lord is risen. . . . If we only have the teaching of Jesus, we have no Gospel. If we only have the account of His perfect life, we have no Gospel. If we only have the Cross, we have no

> Gospel. All these become part of the Gospel because of its central truth, which is that of the resurrection. The deposit, then, the essential and central truth referred to in this phase of the commission, is that of the actual resurrection of Jesus from among the dead.[3]

The point is that those who believe in Jesus Christ must believe in him as a *risen* Savior and not just as a dead Christ.

One of the most tragic examples of the incomplete message of the gospel can be seen near a monastery called Montserrat on a mountain outside of Bogota, Colombia. One can take a cable car to the top of the mountain and then walk through the woods several hundred yards to the monastery. Along the pathway are statues which represent the fourteen stations on the road to the Cross. These are often depicted in the stained glass windows of churches—seven down one side and seven down the other. The fourteen stages represent Christ before Pilate, Christ being taken by the soldiers, Christ carrying his cross, Christ fainting under his cross, Christ hanging on the cross and then being taken from the cross.

After the last statue depicting a dead Christ being removed from the cross there is an actual tomb carved out of the rock of the mountain below the Monastery of Montserrat. The first time I walked along that pathway I was fascinated by the fourteen statues. When I came to the end and saw the tomb I was horrified. Instead of an empty tomb which would depict the glorious truth of the resurrection, in the tomb was a lifesize figure of a dead Christ lying on the slab! This was the end!

What a tragic travesty of the truth of the gospel! As Paul says in 1 Corinthians 15,

> But if there is no resurrection of the dead, then Christ has not been raised; if Christ has not been raised, then our preaching is in vain and your faith is in vain. We are even found to be misrepresenting God, because we testified of God that he raised Christ. . . . If Christ has not been raised,

> your faith is futile and you are still in your sins. (1 Cor. 15:13-15, 17)

But then Paul goes on with the great triumphant outburst:

> But in fact Christ has been raised from the dead, the first fruits of those who have fallen asleep. For as by a man came death, by a man has come also the resurrection of the dead. (1 Cor. 15:20-21)

Yes, the true touchstone of the gospel is the fact that our Savior is alive! Unless Christ actually rose from the dead, Christianity is nothing more than another philosophy propagated by a teacher who died as all other humans die. He claimed to be God. So, if he did not in fact rise from the dead, he was either an imposter or he was deluded. His resurrection is the great proof of his claims to be God incarnate. Thus the whole message of Christianity stands or falls with the resurrection.

When Jesus Christ had upbraided them for their unbelief, emphasizing the fact that he actually was alive, he immediately gave them their responsibility. He told them *where* the gospel is to be preached: "Go into all the world and preach the gospel to the whole creation" (Mk. 16:15).

The word for world, *kosmos*, appears frequently in the New Testament. The basic meaning is, "The orderly universe; the world as the sum total of everything here and now. . . . The creation in its entirety."[4] Morgan refers to this by saying,

> It will thus be seen that the word stands for much more than the people who lived upon the surface of the earth. It refers to the whole earth in its order, its beauty, and its forces. The declaration of the Old Testament "The earth is Jehovah's and the fulness thereof; The world, and they that dwell therein," suggests all that is included in the term "kosmos."[5]

The meaning of the word "creation," *ktisis* is also significant. Arndt and Gingrich define this as, "The sum total of everything created; creation, world."[6] This is consistent with the creation mandate given in Genesis that man is to subdue all the earth and to have dominion over it. It also relates directly to what Paul says in Romans 8 about the whole creation.

> For the creation waits with eager longing for the revealing of the sons of God: for the creation was subjected to futility, not of its own will but by the will of him who subjected it in hope; because the creation itself will be set free from its bondage to decay and obtain the glorious liberty of the children of God. We know that the whole creation has been groaning in travail together until now; and not only the creation, but we ourselves, who have the first fruits of the Spirit, groan inwardly as we wait for adoption as sons, the redemption of our bodies. For in this hope we were saved. Now hope that is seen is not hope. For who hopes for what he sees? But if we hope for what we do not see, we wait for it with patience. (Rom. 8:19-25)

Morgan comments as follows:

> Therefore, the perpetual principle of missionary endeavor is that of passing into the kosmos, and so into the suffering, and thus into ability to communicate renewing forces. . . . The Church must always begin with man, but she must not forget that the emphasis of this commission is that the ultimate result of man's remaking is that of the renewal of the whole creation. . . . That conception of Christian responsibility which aims at the saving of individual men, while it is utterly careless of the groaning of creation, is entirely out of harmony with the meaning of this commission.[7]

It is an encouraging sign in the church around the world today to see many waking up to their responsibility to all of creation. Gregorio Landero is one of the most gifted evangelists I have ever known. As he traveled around in evangelistic outreach to many parts of northern Colombia, he became heavily burdened because the people to whom he was ministering concerning their souls were suffering for lack of nutrition.

He agonized about how he could preach a gospel of salvation when they were starving and suffering diseases which could be avoided with more adequate help. He began to study the possibilities of a more full-orbed outreach of the gospel.

The result, over several years of hard work, was the development of United Action, a program of total outreach for the needs of people. Gregorio is the leader of United Action and has given the vision and impetus to the entire development of the program. Today, along with his evangelistic preaching, he and his colleagues are helping people to improve agricultural methods, developing family poultry projects that will put more protein into their diet, teaching home hygiene, carrying on dental work, literacy work and other things which will develop the family and community life of the people. There have also been efforts to help conserve the natural resources which are a part of the total creation.

These people are demonstrating in a practical way the fulfillment of the Great Commission in concern for the total needs of people. Our understanding of the gospel is deficient unless we see it as ministering to all of creation. Preaching must be accompanied by practical application of the gospel in daily life.

These Signs Will Accompany Those Who Believe

Finally, what are the results of this preaching? Jesus Christ said, "And these signs will accompany those who believe: in my name they will cast out demons; they will speak in new tongues; they will pick up serpents, and if they drink any deadly thing, it will not hurt them; they will lay their hands on the sick, and they will recover" (Mk. 16:17, 18). These signs divide easily into two groups: First, those related to the spiritual realm (casting out demons and speaking in new tongues); and second, those related to the physical realm (picking up serpents, drinking poison and healing the sick).

Jesus is expressing his concern for the physical as well as spiritual welfare of people. For Jesus there was no dichotomy between a spiritual and a physical ministry. He went around preaching, teaching *and* healing. There was never any division either in his mind or in his actions. Thus, when he gave the Great Commission, he included in it the responsibility to minister to the physical as well as to the spiritual needs of all people.

I was sitting on a log in the jungle one day talking to Victor Landero. He had been faithfully preaching the gospel in the entire countryside surrounding his farm. To the best of his ability he was fulfilling the command to preach the gospel to the whole creation. However, he had recently noticed the signs referred to in Mark and was concerned that while they had seen some of the signs, they had not seen all of them. So he asked God why. Up to that time they had seen three out of the five and were expecting any day to see the others as well.

Jesus certainly did not say that every one of these signs would always follow the preaching of the gospel to everyone. In other words, every person who believes will not be expected to pick up serpents nor to drink poison, nor will they necessarily cast out demons or speak in other tongues or heal the sick. In fact, a sign like picking up serpents would be impossible in many areas of the world where no serpents exist. However, these are the types of signs, both physical and spiritual, which will accompany the preaching of the gospel.

It was interesting, nevertheless, to see that Victor Landero, in his simplicity, was expecting God to do exactly what his Word said he would do. He was asking for the confirmation of the message as it was given. And God graciously gave his confirmation to Victor's ministry.

"And they went forth and preached everywhere, while the Lord worked with them and confirmed the message by the signs that attended it" (Mk. 16:20). Thus these signs are for a confirmation of the message. We can expect that God will confirm his message in the ways and at the times that he deems necessary.

The Servant of the Lord and Our Ministry

How does the Commission to reach to the entire creation apply to us today? First, Christ gives us an example. Jesus Christ is the Servant of the Lord. Ours is to be a ministry of service to others. We always see him in Mark active on behalf of other people and in the service of his Father. As Paul put it, "Do nothing from selfishness or conceit, but in humility count others better than yourselves. Let each of you look not only to his own interests, but also to the interests of others" (Phil. 2:3-4). In the rest of Philippians 2 we see that Paul viewed Christ as an example of service which we should emulate.

Christ also gives us the content of our ministry. The resurrection of Jesus Christ is the focus of our entire message. Without the resurrection, the life and death of Jesus become meaningless. Therefore, as Jesus himself emphasized his resurrection and as the apostles preached it fervently in the book of Acts, our ministry must center on the fact that we present a living Savior.

Christ shows us the realm of our ministry. The *kosmos*—the entire creation—is the sphere of our outreach. No single part of the world, neither socially, geographically, politically, economically, racially nor ethnically, is to be left out. There is no person nor place in all of creation which is outside of the love of God and, therefore, outside our responsibility to preach the gospel. This gospel must reach to all of creation in all of its potential. It must minister to the total needs, physical or spiritual, of the human race and the earth itself.

Lastly, Christ gives us the promise for our ministry. Each of the Gospel writers includes a promise in one form or another for those who preach the gospel. Mark includes it indirectly when he states, "And they went forth and preached everywhere, while the Lord worked with them and confirmed the message by the signs that attended it" (Mk. 16:20). As we also obey, going forth and preaching everywhere, the Lord will work with us and confirm the message. "It is when the Church begins to see the suffering of creation with eyes washed by tears, and when she puts herself into such close relation with the wounded world as to share its agony, and as to release her own life blood to heal it, that this commission will be obeyed."[8]

5

In the first book, O Theophilus, I have dealt with all that Jesus began to do and teach, until the day when he was taken up, after he had given commandment through the Holy Spirit to the apostles whom he had chosen. To them he presented himself alive after his passion by many proofs, appearing to them during forty days and speaking of the kingdom of God. And while staying with them he charged them not to depart from Jerusalem, but to wait for the promise of the Father, which, he said, you heard from me, for John baptized with water, but before many days you shall be baptized with the Holy Spirit.

So when they had come together, they asked him, "Lord, will you at this time restore the kingdom to Israel?" He said to them, "It is not for you to know times or seasons which the Father has fixed by his own authority. But you shall receive power when the Holy Spirit has come upon you; and you shall be my witnesses in Jerusalem and in all Judea and Samaria and to the end of the earth." And when he had said this, as they were looking on, he was lifted up, and a cloud took him out of their sight. And while they were gazing into heaven as he went, behold, two men stood by them in white robes, and said, "Men of Galilee, why do you stand looking into heaven? This Jesus, who was taken up from you into heaven, will come in the same way as you saw him go into heaven."

Acts 1:1-11

The Risen Lord Empowers His Church

The book of Acts is a continuation of the gospel narratives. Biblical scholars generally agree the author is Luke. The first sentence makes this clear by referring to "all that Jesus began to do and teach" as recorded previously. This is almost certainly a reference to Luke's Gospel as both Luke and Acts were addressed to a certain Theophilus, of whom we unfortunately know little. Thus, in Acts Luke is continuing a narrative of Jesus begun in the Gospels.

The book of Acts is written in chronological sequence, so it is not difficult to follow the development of the story. It also follows an easily discernible geographic pattern. Acts 1:8 lays the foundation for this by referring to "Jerusalem . . . Judea . . . Samaria . . . the end of the earth." The book can be divided that way for convenience if desired. Acts 1—7 tell how the church continued in Jerusalem the work that Jesus had begun. Acts 8—12 center in Judea and Samaria as well as Jerusalem, with the start of reaching out to other areas also indicated. Then Acts 13—28 describe the more full development of the outreach toward the end of the earth. In 13:1-3 the Holy Spirit calls Paul and Barnabas to move out beyond Antioch on the first of the great missionary journeys that occupy most of the rest of Acts.

With this general context in mind we now can analyze more closely the Commission as found at the outset of this book.

Jesus' Last Words

The last three verses of the introduction to Acts make it clear that verse eight includes the last words that Jesus Christ ever spoke to his disciples. He chose for those last words to repeat once again the Great Commission which he also gave among his first words after the resurrection. We noticed in Luke and John that the first time Jesus met with his disciples following the resurrection, he explained the necessity that they be witnesses to all nations. He repeated that at least once the same evening. He repeated it later on the mountain in Galilee as recorded in Matthew 28. And now he is outside the city of Jerusalem, forty days later, just before his ascension.

He Presented Himself Alive

He knows that his disciples will remember—perhaps longer than anything else he ever said—the last words that come from his lips. And so he chooses them carefully. "You are to be my witnesses . . . to the end of the earth" (Acts 1:8).

In analyzing the passage we find, first of all, the premise for world missions. Luke tells Theophilus that in his Gospel he dealt with "all that Jesus began to do and teach, until the day when he was taken up, after he had given commandment through the Holy Spirit to the apostles whom he had chosen. To them he presented himself alive after his passion by many proofs" (Acts 1:1-3). He presented himself *alive*. The resurrection of Jesus Christ becomes the indispensable basis of the entire world mission of the church. Johannes Blauw puts it this way: "It is clear that the resurrection as the crowning of

Christ's work is *the* first and great presupposition and condition for the proclamation of the gospel among the nations."[1] Georg Vicedom describes it this way:

> Accordingly the resurrection is the necessary antecedent of the sending, the *conditio sine qua non*, from which the apostles receive their commission.... This fact has such a strong impact that in the apostolic preaching it is not the cross, but the resurrection which always occupies the central position. It is the decisive fact.[2]

Only when there is resurrection does the cross take on significance. For that reason, above all else, mission work is founded on the resurrection without which Jesus would not be the redeemer of the world.

Thus the Great Commission rests primarily on the fact that we serve a living Savior who sends us into the world with the message that he has risen from the dead. The worst twisting of the truth of Christianity is that which presents Jesus as a dead Christ rather than as a living Lord.

There is a village in the mountains of Guatemala called Chichicastenango where one can witness a classic example of the syncretism between the ancient pagan religions of Latin America and so-called Christianity. Chichicastenango is an Indian village whose roots go back to the Mayan Empire. Many of the traditions and religious rituals practiced centuries ago, long before the coming of Christianity to that area, are still being practiced.

Ascending the steps of one of the churches in that village, one can see the Indian witchdoctors swinging their censers and intoning incantations in their native languages. Inside the church along the aisle you will see them lighting candles before images whose names have been changed. They are still worshiping the ancient Mayan gods that now carry Christian names.

In the front of the church is a large glass coffin. Inside is a life-size figure of a beaten, bloody, dead Christ. I have watched the Indians go up the aisle on their knees lighting candle after candle reciting their incantations. Then they come up to this glass coffin and kiss it. I have stood there and wondered to myself, "What in the world is going on in the mind of this Indian, whose ancestry goes back into the paganism of the Mayan Empire, as he kisses the glass coffin of a dead, defeated, broken Christ?" The tragedy is that this is the only picture they have. No concept of resurrection. No message of hope.

By contrast, in the city of Guatemala there is a large modern Roman Catholic church. The first thing one sees on walking into this church, instead of the traditional crucifix or a dead, defeated Christ in a glass coffin, is a magnificent statue of the risen Christ ascending to heaven. Around him the apostles are watching him ascend. It is a dramatic demonstration of the truth of the resurrection of Jesus Christ.

I saw those two churches on two succeeding days and was impressed with the contrast which brings forth the message of the resurrection. This is the theme of the preaching of the apostles in Acts. It is the basis on which the Great Commission was given.

You Shall Receive Power

Jesus told them to wait for the promise of the Father, then to get busy. At this point the disciples became preoccupied with the question of timing. They wondered whether the kingdom was coming now. They asked, "Lord will you at this time restore the kingdom to Israel?" (Acts 1:6). Jesus replied, "It is not for you to know times or seasons which the Father has fixed by his own authority. But . . . you shall be my witnesses" (Acts 1:7-8). He was saying, in effect, "You are not to know those things. But there is something you must know. You are to get busy with the job that I give you. Don't get sidetracked with things like the timing of the Last Days."

Today there is a strong emphasis in some quarters on eschatology. This can be healthy. But I must confess to some uneasiness about an overemphasis on prophecy. Today some seem to be perilously close to setting dates again for the coming of Christ. The church has been through such phases before, and it can lead to disillusionment. I was a boy during the late thirties. I can remember the prophetic preaching that was so popular at that time. During the summer of 1939 just prior to the outbreak of World War 2 almost everyone was preaching on prophecy. They were announcing the coming holocaust that was about to engulf the world. The antichrist was here. There was some disagreement as to who he was. But he was certainly here. Mussolini seemed to be the front runner at the time. Stalin was not far behind. Hitler seemed to be a little farther behind the two of them. But if the antichrist wasn't one, he certainly was another of those three. On September 1 when World War 2 broke out, we were told this was the beginning of the end. Armageddon was just around the corner. The coming of the Lord was at hand.

As a young boy I was so impressed with this preaching that I really believed we would never see the year 1940. I didn't see how we could make it through those months into the next decade. I remember waking on the 1st of January 1940 with a great sigh, wondering what in the world had happened!

The Lord reminds us, "It is not for you to know times or seasons which the Father has fixed by his own authority." What, then, am I supposed to know? "You shall receive power when the Holy Spirit has come upon you; and you shall be my witnesses in Jerusalem and in all Judea and Samaria and to the end of the earth." That power which is indispensable in the fulfillment of our mission is promised. Blauw puts it, "The close connection with the call to mission and Holy Spirit cannot be exaggerated."[3]

We cannot overestimate the necessity of the power of the Holy Spirit in the ministry to which God calls us. It was noted previously that Harry Boer in *Pentecost and Missions* develops biblically and irrefutably that the coming of the Holy Spirit, the Pentecost experience, gives life and meaning to the Great Commission. The Great Commission without Pentecost could have no power and could not be fulfilled. But the coming of the Holy Spirit makes it possible to carry out the command. As the resurrection is the indispensable element in the message of the gospel, the Pentecost experience is the indispensable element of empowering Christ's disciples to carry that message to the ends of the earth.

It is exciting to see men and women respond in the power of the Holy Spirit and preach the gospel because they have met the Lord. Whether they have understood the Great Commission or not, when the power of the Holy Spirit grips them, they begin to witness.

One night I was preaching in a small church in Cartagena, Colombia. Halfway through the message I noticed a man come in and sit down in the back row. He seemed to be a bit inebriated, and I discovered later that he was.

Following the benediction he came up to me unsteadily and said, "I have come looking for the salvation of my soul." Now I was a little skeptical, as he was obviously under the influence of liquor. I was not sure that he knew what he was saying. But one can't turn away a seeking man on that basis. So I sat down with Agustín and discussed the meaning of the gospel. He professed that night to receive Jesus Christ.

We went home on furlough shortly after that so I didn't see Agustin again until we returned to Colombia eight or nine months later. I found that he was now an active participant in the church. He had led his wife and his father to the Lord and was witnessing to others.

He then told me the full story of why he had come to church

that night. He said, "I had reached the point of desperation. I had come to the end of my rope. I was living with fourteen women at the same time. [His wife confirmed this for me.] I was trying to support my family, but I was drinking up all that I earned. I would get drunk with the money from my weekly paycheck and get into fights every weekend. Finally, in desperation I told my wife, 'I am walking out of this house, and I am not coming back until I find the salvation of my soul.' I walked down the streets of Cartagena. I passed that church and saw someone preaching. I went in and sat down, and that is when I came up to you."

How thankful I was that I had not allowed my skepticism to overrule that night. He was genuinely seeking salvation. I had no opportunity at that time to teach him any further, and no one else really gave him much teaching. But the Holy Spirit undertook for him.

Agustín later led his friend Roberto to Christ. Roberto led his wife to the Lord. His wife then led to Christ her sister who, in turn, led her husband, Ramón to the Lord. While preparing this book I received a letter from Colombia informing me that Ramón had now become the coordinator of all the work in northern Colombia that had grown out of the efforts of the Latin America Mission.

Ramón was the fifth spiritual generation from Agustín. Each one, under the power of the Holy Spirit, had accepted the responsibility to be a witness. We rejoice in the work of the Holy Spirit that took hold in the lives of those people. Blauw says that Acts 1:8 could just as well be translated, "You shall receive the power of the Holy Spirit *in order to* be my witnesses."[4]

Witnesses to the End of the Earth

Jesus then outlined the pattern for witness. It is from Jerusalem, to Judea, to Samaria and to the end of the earth.

Nothing is left out. We must start where we are. But we don't stop there.

Notice that the Lord chose that little word *and* rather than the conjunction *or*. Had he chosen the word *or* this verse could read: "You start out in Jerusalem. Or (if things don't go well there) another option would be Judea. Or (if you can't make it in Judea) you can always try Samaria. Or (as a last resort) there are always the ends of the earth." But he did not use the word *or*. He chose the word *and* putting them all on an equal plane. There is no distinction between Jerusalem and the ends of the earth in the Lord's mind. Every part of the world must be reached. We have no option. Our responsibility is from Jerusalem to the end of the earth.

Just before we left Colombia, Victor Landero invited me to make a farewell trip in the backwoods area. "You have been here with us for years, and we have worked together. Now let's make a trip and visit the churches one more time before you leave." I was thrilled with this invitation. We spent about two weeks together. We went from village to village where there was a growing movement—scores of believers in one church, hundreds in another and dozens of churches all over the area.

During that time I kept thinking about my brother Phil and how in the same year that we went to Latin America he headed up into northern Canada. In fourteen years he had not seen one convert. In that same period of time God had allowed us to watch a great turning to the Lord in Colombia. I kept asking, "Lord, why is it that you take two brothers and send one off to no results of any sort and you allow the other to watch a great in-gathering? Lord, why don't you let Phil see even one convert? Couldn't you let him have one?"

The Lord seemed to say to me one night, "Dave, why don't you share this with these Colombians? These people really know how to pray." It was true. I have never seen people that love to pray the way they do. If someone wakes up at one o'clock in the morning and feels like praying, he will get out of his hammock and pray. I have heard them do it. I have slept in homes with bamboo walls and could hear what was going on in the next room. They may pray for a half hour and go back to bed. Five o'clock in the morning is a common time for prayer meetings. Four-thirty prayer meetings are not uncommon. Nor is it uncommon to walk through the woods and hear a farmer singing and praying in the middle of the day as he plants his corn. It is not uncommon to hear a woman preparing a meal in her house and just stop for a while, kneel down on the dirt floor of her little kitchen and pray for a few moments. When I would arrive in one of these villages after a trek through the woods, the immediate greeting would always be the same. The first Christians I would meet would say, "Welcome Don David. Glad to see you. Now let's pray." Then they would thank the Lord for bringing me safely there.

So one night instead of giving the Bible study that I had prepared, I spoke informally for about a half hour about my brother Phil. I told how we had grown up together as boys and how the Lord had led him to the frozen expanses of northern Canada and had brought me down to Colombia. I described how in those years when we were seeing a great work of the Holy Spirit, he worked so hard and had seen the opposition of Satan but had never seen any breakthrough. "You people here have seen God overcome Satan." (This was an area where there had been great satanic opposition. They had struggled with demon powers. They knew how to pray and break through.) "Maybe God wants the church in Colombia to share in establishing the church in northern Canada." Then I sat down.

The leader rose and said, "I think we should go to prayer right now." He didn't have to repeat the invitation. Two hundred people went to their knees immediately and began to pray. Their custom is for all to pray out loud together. The reason is not that they are "holy rollers" or that they want a lot of shouting. Not at all. It is simply that when someone comes to a prayer meeting, he comes to pray, not to listen to someone else pray. So everyone prays aloud together. That evening they prayed for one hour and fifteen minutes without stopping. They poured out their hearts for Phil and his wife Margaret and for those Canadian Indians.

At one point the lay pastor and his wife came over, laid hands on me and prayed forcefully for Phil. The next day the pastor's wife apologized for doing that. I said, "I don't quite understand your apology."

"Well, we don't do that kind of thing here. Men lay hands on men and women on women, but not women on men. I think I owe you an apology."

"There is certainly no offense. I never thought of such a thing."

Then she said, "Let me tell you why I did it though. I was so burdened in my heart for Phil that I just had to lay hands on him in prayer. You were the closest I could get to him, so I laid hands on you."

The next day two people in the village brought me letters written to Phil asking that I send them to him. So I translated them into English and sent them up to Phil. They were letters of encouragement, telling him of their support in prayer and exhorting him to take heart.

The next morning I awoke at five o'clock to hear the pastor and his wife in the next room get up. I heard them pray aloud for an hour. The first thing they prayed for was Phil, his wife and those Indians in Canada.

We came home on furlough the following month. That summer Phil invited us to Canada to speak to his mission. So we went. Our two families had a great time together. While we were there Phil's wife said to me, "Dave, back in April Phil had reached the lowest point in morale that I have ever seen him have in all of our fourteen years in Canada. He was closer to quitting than I have ever seen him before. Every night he would go to bed defeated and discouraged. He would get up in the morning and drag himself out of bed. He had no joy, no real faith to believe and was feeling, 'After fourteen years, what's the use? We might as well quit and go somewhere else.'

"One night he went to bed as defeated and discouraged as ever. The next morning he got up a totally new man. We didn't know what had happened. He had great joy. He had new faith. He had new courage to go on and believe that God was going to work. Then we received those letters that you had sent up. I checked the dates and, of course, that was the night that those Colombians were praying for him."

Now there wasn't an immediate breakthrough and no great people movement to report. He still waited another couple of years before he saw the first convert. But periodically my Colombian friends would ask by letter, "Tell us about Don Felipe. How is he doing? We are praying for him."

I would reply, "Keep praying."

Finally Phil asked me, on a trip to the United States, "Dave, are your Colombian friends still praying for us?"

"Yes, they are."

Then he told me how the Spirit of God was beginning to work. It was not a great people movement yet, but by ones and twos they were coming to Christ. These were the beginnings of a church. So I wrote to my Colombian brethren and told them. They wrote back, "Yes, we knew it. It was just a matter of time, but we knew it was going to happen."

These Colombians have taken northern Canada as their "ends of the earth." Probably none of them will ever get there. But they have participated in extending the body of Christ to that region.

I want to be present when those Canadian Indians meet those Colombian Christians in heaven for the first time. It is going to be a beautiful scene. The Indians came to Jesus Christ because a group of peasants in Colombia prayed for them.

This Jesus Will Come

Finally, after Jesus Christ had given this command, he was taken up into heaven. The disciples, having seen him go, stood there in perplexity. Suddenly two men stood beside them and said, "Men of Galilee, why do you stand looking into heaven? This Jesus, who was taken up from you into heaven, will come in the same way as you saw him go into heaven" (Acts 1:11).

The hope of world missions is the coming of Jesus Christ. The giving of the Great Commission by Jesus Christ is set between the resurrection and Pentecost. The implementation of the Great Commission is set between Pentecost and the coming of Jesus Christ. And that is our great hope.

Hope is indispensable for human life and activity to flourish. When hope is removed, spirits die and meaningful action becomes impossible.

Recently my family and I visited the infamous concentration camp in Dachau, Germany. We entered the gates and saw the barbed wire fences, the moats, the guard towers all calculated to make escape well nigh impossible. We proceeded through the stark barracks where thousands of humans had been herded like cattle on their way to the ominous gas chambers which stand at a far end of the camp. I was reminded of Dante's famous lines as he described arriving at the gates of Hell and seeing the forbidding inscription:

> Through me you pass into the city of woe;
> Through me you pass into eternal pain;
> Through me among the people lost for aye. . . .
> All hope abandon, ye who enter here.[5]

We wandered in stunned silence through the museum at

Dachau where the whole history of that tragic period is depicted with huge photographs and other terrifying mementos of man's inhumanity to man. Four pictures in particular caught my eye and I found myself studying each one in depth.

The first showed a large crowd of Jews being marched to the gas chambers. One man was too weak to walk, so he was being dragged over the shoulder of a companion. His hollow eyes were staring blankly into space, his mouth hung open, his limbs hung limp. The awesome sense of hopelessness in his face was almost too much to contemplate.

The second picture showed a massive open grave, with hundreds of tangled bodies piled indiscriminately on top of each other. All hope was gone for these victims.

The third picture, displayed toward the end of the museum hallway, was a startling contrast. Hundreds of prisoners had suddenly overcome their hopeless stupor. They were leaping up with shouts of joy. Arms were raised in ecstasy. Men were climbing on anything available to get a better look. Allied troops had just burst into the camp to liberate these hopeless creatures from certain death. Hope had suddenly revived! There was new life for them!

But the fourth was again a tragic reminder of how all hope was gone for some. An American soldier was stooping by a wall of the camp. Skeletal bodies with those gnawing faces of death were piled against the wall in what appeared to be a futile attempt to escape at the last moment. The look on the face of the GI was one of horrified incredulity. His mouth hung open in disbelief, his eyes reflected terror and sadness. He had arrived too late to help some. Hope was gone for them.

The message of Jesus Christ is a message of hope. It is a message of life. And when he commanded his disciples to proclaim this message to all the world, he gave them the hope that would keep them going. John Gardner has said, "The first and last task of a leader is to keep hope alive."[6] Jesus Christ did this by the great promise of his return. As his church moves out in obedience to his command, it does so with the promise of his final victory upon earth, when he returns to reign and "the kingdom of the world has become the kingdom of our Lord and of his Christ, and he shall reign for ever and ever" (Rev. 11:15).

This gospel must be preached among all nations and *then* shall the end come (Mt. 24:14). When you and I, as members of the body of Christ, have responded in obedience in sending this gospel to the ends of the earth, then, and only then, this same Jesus whom they saw taken up into heaven, will come again to earth.

An Overview

The Son of Man focused on the Great Commission in Luke by putting it into the context of the whole history of redemption beginning with Genesis. Jesus Christ took his disciples back into the books of Moses, the psalms and the prophets. Then he said, "Now the next step is for *you* to be my witnesses."

Having brought them up to date with the history of redemption, the Son of God in the book of John sent his church. "As the Father sent me, even so I send you." That is, "You are the future of God's redemptive history."

In Matthew the King of kings proclaimed his authority and dominion by saying that "all authority is mine; therefore, as you go, make disciples of all nations in my name, teaching them everything that I have taught you."

In Mark the Servant of the Lord defined our ministry in terms of the *kosmos.* There is no part of creation that is outside the realm of our responsibility. We must meet the physical as well as the spiritual needs of mankind in the entire *kosmos.*

Finally, as we have seen in Acts, the risen Savior empowered his church.

That is the Great Commission for today. That is the way it was given and that is the way it stands. Notice again the emphasis which Jesus Christ placed upon it. He gave it at least four times. He gave it twice the opening night. He gave it again in Galilee on a mountain. And he gave it just before ascending to heaven. His disciples could not miss the importance that he was placing on this task that was now theirs.

Today the church stands between Pentecost and the Second Coming. Our responsibility is to make the gospel known in all of its fulness and power to the ends of the earth.

Let every kindred, every tribe,
On this terrestrial ball,
To Him all majesty ascribe,
And crown Him Lord of all.

Questions for Discussion

If we are honest with ourselves about the implications of discipleship, of following Jesus Christ, we must grapple with what Christ says about the world mission of the church. One way to do this is through a group discussion of the present book.

The following questions are designed to help a group move through some of the relevant issues. There are five studies, one for each chapter of the book. Each fits comfortably in a 60-minute time slot. The members of the group should read each chapter before coming to the discussion.

The questions provide a skeleton on which to hang discussion. This allows the leader freedom to adapt each study to the flow of discussion through follow-up questions and the like. Scattered throughout are application questions which personalize the discussion and keep it from constantly being theoretical.

Each study is divided into thought units, indicated by the rules across the page. Although summary questions are provided only at the end for the entire book, after each discussion the leader is encouraged to summarize the main points the group has brought out.

A leader need not have "all the answers" but rather should lead the people in the group to discover for themselves what is involved in the Great Commission. (Helpful general suggestions for leading group discussions are found in James Nyquist's *Leading Bible Discussions,* especially chapter eight. This is available from InterVarsity Press.)

Preface and Chapter One

☐ What first comes to your mind when you hear the word *missions?*

☐ Why is it important to know what the Bible says about missions?

☐ What does Howard mean by saying that in missions "obedience to the Word of God becomes the issue" (p. 11)?

☐ What are some of the Old Testament passages referred to in chapter one that show God's concern for the whole world?

☐ Do you *feel* as if God is concerned for the whole world? Where do you see his concern? Where don't you see it?

☐ Discuss this sentence: "God permits persecution or perhaps some kind of tragedy to force the issue" of obeying the Great Commission (p. 21). Do you agree?

☐ Have you ever been persecuted? for your faith? What resulted from it?

☐ How does Luke emphasize Christ's own manhood?

☐ How does Luke emphasize Christ's concern for humanity? What evidence is there in Luke that "Jesus moved out to all elements of society"?

☐ What groups are you isolated from?

☐ What social barriers stop you or your fellowship group from sharing the gospel? What emotional barriers are there as well? (Fear? Lack of understanding? Feeling uncomfortable?)

☐ What concrete steps can you take to remove the causes of separation?

☐ Howard says, "There can be no question that this [Jesus' statement, 'You are witnesses of these things'] applies to the whole church of Jesus Christ" (p. 30). What are the advantages and disadvantages of having only trained people do the witnessing? What are the advantages and disadvantages of having all Christians (no matter what training they may have) do the witnessing?

Chapter Two

☐ Apparently, Christ gave the Great Commission twice on his first meeting with the disciples. Why does Christ say the same thing twice in two different ways?

☐ What was John's purpose in writing his Gospel?

☐ How do the seven miracles in John show Christ as the Son of God?

☐ What is the secondary organization in the Gospel of John?

☐ How does it make you feel to know that the Son of God sees you as an individual and not just as part of a crowd? Does this make you want to respond in any particular way?

☐ "As we carry out the Great Commission, we dare not lose sight of that personal touch which Jesus Christ so desperately wants" (p. 37). Why? What is so important about it?

☐ Have you ever witnessed impersonally, as the missionary did with the American couple who lost their two-month-old child? What should have been done instead?

☐ Do you think it's true that "others will not come to know Christ if they don't see love within us" (p. 42)?

☐ What is the *work* of God? To what degree should we do this work for him (that is, to make other people believe)?

☐ What is the place of forgiveness in the gospel message?

☐ In what ways did Eliecer experience forgiveness?

☐ In what ways have you experienced God's forgiveness?
☐ Think of those things you most regret having done. Can you forgive yourself for them? If not, does this hamper you from forgiving others? from offering Christ's forgiveness to others?

Chapter Three

☐ What does this statement mean: "Worship and doubt are not nearly so far apart from each other as one might expect" (p. 58)?
☐ How are worship of Christ and doubt about him connected?
☐ How are worship of Christ and obedience to him connected?
☐ Contrast doubt and unbelief.
☐ Do you have doubts about Christianity that are unresolved? If so, what are you doing to work through these?

☐ How is Christ's kingship emphasized in Matthew?
☐ What characteristics of a king come to mind? How would you act around a king?
☐ What does Christ's authority have to do with the Great Commission?
☐ How can Christ's authority give you comfort and assurance as you go with the gospel?

☐ Christ said, "Go therefore and make disciples of all nations." What else is involved in making disciples besides bringing people to Christ?
☐ How would you help a new Christian grow in his walk with God? (What books, seminars, groups of people, activities would you get him involved in?)
☐ What kind of time commitment do you suppose would be necessary on your part?

☐ What are the four "alls" of the Great Commission?

☐ What do you know about Bible smuggling? What ethical issues are involved?
☐ Is it within the rights of a Christian to break a law to bring the Bible to people?
☐ When is it right for a Christian to break the law to spread the gospel? When is it not right?

Chapter Four
☐ How is Christ's servanthood emphasized in Mark?
☐ Consider Mark 10:45: "For the Son of man also came not to be served but to serve, and to give his life a ransom for many." How are a servant and a king different? How are they alike?
☐ What is the importance of the resurrection in the gospel message? in your life?

☐ In Mark 16 what does Christ say the extent of our responsibility is? Does this include more than the souls of all people?
☐ What was Christ's example for us in this regard? Why was he concerned with physical as well as with spiritual needs? Do you find yourself thinking of them separately?
☐ Do people have other needs besides spiritual and physical ones? Are we responsible to deal with these as well?
☐ Love has been defined as active concern for another's best. How did Christ show love in his earthly ministry?

Chapter Five
☐ How much emphasis should be placed on eschatology (study of the last times)?
☐ What seems to be Jesus' view in Acts 1?
☐ What was Jesus concerned about in Acts 1?

☐ "We cannot overestimate the necessity of the power of the Holy Spirit in the ministry to which God calls us" (p. 96). What does this mean?
☐ What is the Holy Spirit's role as we spread the gospel? What is our role?
☐ What is the importance of prayer in world evangelism? in home evangelism?
☐ How much are you involved in prayer for others?
☐ What reasons are there for your level of involvement in prayers?

☐ What is hope?
☐ What, according to Howard, is the hope of world missions (p. 102)? Why is this so?
☐ Why do the angels mention Christ's return to the disciples?
☐ How does his return affect your life and living now? What motivation does it offer?

Summary
☐ What comes to mind *now* when you hear the word *mission?* How, if at all, has your reaction changed from before you read this book?
☐ What have you learned about who Christ is? How has that affected your attitude toward world missions?

Notes

chapter one

[1]J. H. Bavinck, *An Introduction to the Science of Missions* (Grand Rapids, Michigan: Baker, 1960), p. 12.

[2]Merrill C. Tenney, *The New Testament: An Historical and Analytic Survey* (Grand Rapids, Michigan: Wm. B. Eerdmans, 1953), p. 193.

chapter two

[1]Johannes Blauw, *The Missionary Nature of the Church* (New York: McGraw-Hill, 1962), p. 88.

[2]Merrill C. Tenney, *John: The Gospel of Belief* (Grand Rapids, Michigan: Wm. B. Eerdmans, 1948), pp. 30-31.

[3]D. Guthrie, J. A. Motyer, *The New Bible Commentary: Revised* (Downers Grove, Illinois: InterVarsity Press, 1970), p. 966.

chapter three

[1]Blauw, pp. 85-86.

[2]Karl Barth, "An Exegetical Study of Matthew 28:16-20," in *The Theology of the Christian Mission*, by Gerald H. Anderson, ed. (New York: McGraw-Hill, 1961), p. 58.

[3]Everett F. Harrison, "Worship" in *Baker's Dictionary of Theology*, ed., Everett F. Harrison (Grand Rapids, Michigan: Baker, 1960), p. 560.

[4]Barth, p. 60.

[5]Alfred Tennyson, "In Memoriam," in *The Poetical Works of Alfred Tennyson* (New York: Houghton Mifflin, n.d.), p. 312.

[6]*The New Bible Handbook*, ed. G. T. Manley (Chicago: InterVarsity Press, 1949), pp. 323-24.

[7]W. F. Arndt and F. W. Gingrich, *A Greek-English Lexicon of the New Testament* (Chicago: The University of Chicago Press, 1957), p. 277.

[8]John R. W. Stott, "The Great Commission," in *One Race, One Gospel, One Task*, I, ed. Carl F. H. Henry and W. Stanley Mooneyham (Minneapolis: Worldwide Publications, 1967), p. 45.

[9]Ibid., p. 36.

[10]Blauw, p. 86.

[11]Barth, pp. 64-65.

chapter four

[1]Tenney, *The New Testament*, p. 176.

[2]Eusebius, *Ecclesiastical History*, III. 39, quoted in *The Zondervan Pictorial Encyclopedia of the Bible*, ed. M. C. Tenney (Grand Rapids, Michigan: Zondervan, 1975), IV, p. 77.

[3]G. Campbell Morgan, *The Missionary Manifesto* (Grand Rapids, Michigan: Baker, 1970), pp. 64-65.

[4]Arndt and Gingrich, p. 446.

[5]Morgan, p. 70.

[6]Arndt and Gingrich, p. 457.

[7]Morgan, pp. 76-78.

[8]Ibid., p. 81.

chapter five

[1]Blauw, pp. 88-89.

[2]Georg F. Vicedom, *The Mission of God* (St. Louis: Concordia, 1965), pp. 58-59.

[3]Blauw, p. 89.

[4]Ibid., p. 90.

[5]Dante, *The Divine Comedy* (New York: E. P. Dutton, 1908), pp. 9-10.

[6]John W. Gardner, *No Easy Victories* (New York: Harper and Row, 1968), p. 134.